"THERE'S ONE AWAY"
Escapes from Dartmoor Prison

DEDICATION

With love and gratitude to Kathleen Mary Rose James — my Mother, who first inspired my interest in Dartmoor and the prison.

Illustrations pages 35. 50. 54. 55. Brian Steffens

First published in Great Britain in 1999

Copyright © Trevor James 1999

ISBN 1 898964 36 X

Orchard Publications
2 Orchard Close, Chudleigh, Newton Abbot, Devon TQ13 0LR
Telephone: (01626) 852714

Printed by
Hedgerow Print
The Old Creamery, Lapford, Crediton, Devon EX17 6AE

FOREWORD

An indomitable spirit leads a small number of prisoners to attempt to escape, a tiny handful successfully. This book recalls a few which occurred from Dartmoor Prison in this and the last Century.

It is a fascinating account of single-mindedness, planning, and execution, occasionally linked with ruthless actions.

Any escape leads to an examination of security practices, and subsequent change to prevent repetition.

Hopefully there will be no more from Dartmoor Prison; a fine staff will ensure the protection of the community.

JOHN LAWRENCE
GOVERNOR
DARTMOOR PRISON

ACKNOWLEDGEMENTS

I wish to thank Mr J. Lawrence, Governor of Dartmoor Prison, for his generous help and for very kindly taking time from a busy schedule to write a Foreword.

Among the many friends, acquaintances and colleagues who assisted with this book by providing local knowledge, anecdotes and pictures are the following past and present members of staff of H.M.P. Dartmoor: Mr J. Conduit (Director of Works); Principal Officer D. Pinhey; Principal Officer G. Harris (Rtd.); Senior Officer J. Dunne; Senior Officer A. Palmer (Rtd.); Prison Officer Mike Chamberlain; Prison Officer B. Easterbrook I.S.M. (Rtd.) and Mr B. Johnson (Curator, Dartmoor Prison Museum).

Officers, past and present, of the Devon and Cornwall Constabulary, who kindly answered queries and supplied material, included: Superintendent D.Roper (Retd.) and Mrs Roper; Sergeant K. Northey (Retd.); Sgt. P. Broad (Retd.); Constable R. Borlase (Rtd.) and Constable K. James (Rtd.). Special thanks to Constable S. Dell M.B.E. for his more than generous contributions.

I am also grateful to: Mr B. Estill (Curator, Devon and Cornwall Constabulary Museum, Exeter); Mr M. Ware (Curator, National Motor Museum, Beaulieu, Hants); Mr D. German (formerly of Princetown) and Mr C. Waycott (Princetown) for information and pictures.

CONTENTS

AUTHOR'S PREFACE

The first convict prisoners arrived at Dartmoor on 2 November 1850. On the 10 December the first escape occurred when three men absconded, and it's been going on ever since. An escape-proof prison has not yet been built and probably never will be. The design and remote locations of the most secure jails in the world have failed to match the ingenuity of their inmates, who have overcome seemingly impossible obstacles and escaped. The most notorious of them, the island prison of Alcatraz in America, and the French penal establishment in the jungles of South America, which included the infamous 'Devil's Island' (both are now defunct), failed to confine their prisoners with total effectiveness.

The history of Dartmoor prison has a liberal sprinkling of escape stories, some of them more exciting than any work of fiction and so daringly executed even the authorities had a grudging admiration for the boldness and bravery of the prisoners involved in them. Sadly, many men have sought, and found, the most certain method of escape — suicide. It still happens. Others have involuntarily 'escaped' into insanity. The public, who generally view escapees with alarm, have in the past often extended sympathy to them when they were caught, congregating to witness their return to custody amid cheering and shouts of encouragement as if they were heroes. It cannot be denied a romantic aura surrounds the spectacle of a man on the run (Great Train Robber 'Ronnie' Biggs is a classic example), and a 'sporting' atmosphere has often been apparent on the moor when the latest sighting of a runaway, news of a housebreak, or when clothes have been stolen and kitchens raided for food, were discussed in Dartmoor pubs with a light-heartedness certainly not shared by the victims. Members of the public are often puzzled about the meaning of the various categories of prisoners. There are four categories, A B C and D, each of which is directly related to an individual's escape potential:
Category A.
Those who have the support and the means (possibly on the outside) for escape, or represent a threat to the public. These type of prisoners are confined in 'high security' prisons.
Category B.
Are a high escape risk but do not have the means.
Category C.
Are not a high escape or security risk, but may be 'opportunists'.
Category D.
Represent no risk whatsoever either of escaping or being a threat to the public.
Categories B C and D are confined in Dartmoor prison today.

Apart from the gangster types held at Dartmoor in the past whose motives for escape were far from sentimental, most escapees have a domestic problem or concern about a wife or girlfriend. Until recently a prisoner could clear his debts to other inmates by escaping or attempting to escape. An example of this happened some years ago at Channings Wood prison, near Newton Abbot, when an inmate successfully absconded, and when he was clear of the prison calmly waited by the roadside for a lift back! A prison officer on his way to work kindly obliged. Then there are the 'opportunists' who see a chance to escape and take it there and then. Once they are out they are often at a loss as to what to do. One man who ran away from the prison farm in 1995 was recognised and apprehended by an off-duty officer in Tavistock who saw him aimlessly walking the streets looking in shop windows.

What happens to recaptured prisoners? When Dartmoor was a War Prison (1809-1815) French and American escapees were locked up for ten days in the 'Black Hole', a 20 ft square dungeon without heating or bedding, and on two thirds of their normal rations. If the military guards aided their escape those concerned

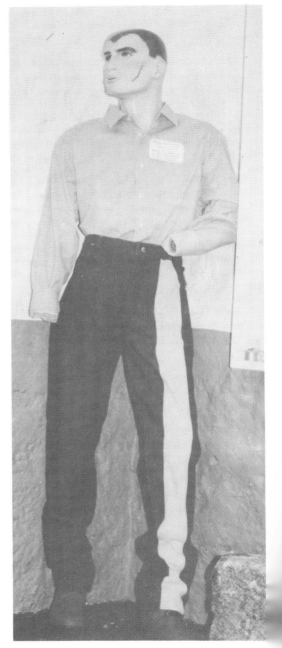

'E' List prisoners' distinctive clothing.
(Author's photo) — Courtesy of Dartmoor Prison Museum

faced a Court Martial and were sometimes shot; a flogging was the mildest punishment they could expect. A civilian helping an escapee got a public whipping, a term in the pillory, or transportation to the Colonies. Apprehending a prisoner who escaped brought a £5 reward and this practice continued well into the 20th century.

In the Victorian convict era a recaptured prisoner was punished by being placed in heavy chains and/or on a restricted diet (three days bread and water only). The warders were charged with neglect of duty which resulted in a fine, reduction in rank, or loss of seniority. These days escapees are placed in solitary confinement until they are seen by the Governor who may award them up to 42 days loss of remission. They then spend six months on what is called the 'E' list which entails strict precautions being taken to prevent them escaping again. Their presence is checked at intervals day and night, and they are escorted everywhere they go inside the prison. They wear distinctive clothing with a yellow stripe on the trouser legs, are allocated specially selected cells, and at night their clothes and eating utensils are taken from them leaving them just their night attire. Offences committed by them whilst at large are dealt with by the local Magistrates in the normal way and an additional sentence may result; in any case 'time out' does not count towards their existing sentence.

Escaping from prison is a very unattractive business but it is always going to happen and each incident brings its individual element of drama and excitement. Of the scores of prisoners who have gone 'over the wall' since Dartmoor accepted its first prisoner in 1809, some have been killed in the attempt; most of them were recaptured; all of them found the wide and lonely moor their most formidable guardian.

DARTMOOR PRISON

The prison was built during the war with Napoleon (1803–1814) to accommodate French prisoners of war previously held aboard the hulks (redundant men of war converted for use as floating prisons) anchored off Plymouth. They were badly overcrowded and the death rate was unacceptably high, which is why, with the number of prisoners taken continuing to rise, extra war prisons were required and Prince's Town, as it was first called, was one of the approved sites. Sir Thomas Tyrwhitt, who founded Princetown, laid the Foundation Stone and the prison opened on 24 May 1809.

Two circular boundary walls nearly a mile in circumference enclosed five prison blocks, a hospital and a separate prison for the officers. Each block had three floors, two of which were of concrete and provided with rows of iron posts for the slinging of hammocks — no hardship involved here as most of the captives at this time were sailors. The wooden top floor was for exercise in bad weather, but as the prison filled to capacity it became a dormitory too and 1500 men were crammed into buildings designed to hold just 1000. There were no windows, only a series of 2 ft. square apertures for ventilation, and no heating; the body heat of the mass of close-packed men kept them alive in the depth of winter, but the fetid atmosphere it created was the cause of disease, typhoid for example, and chest complaints. By the year 1813, as a result of British military successes in the Peninsula campaign, Dartmoor was severely overcrowded. There were now more than 10,000 prisoners in a prison originally intended for 5,000 despite the fact two extra blocks were constructed in 1811, and when the Americans began arriving in 1813 (mostly sailors captured during the War of 1812) the overcrowding got worse.

Their recreation was gambling and manufacturing model ships, trinkets, and various knick-knacks for barter at the market which was held each day within the prison where local traders sold poultry, vegetables, tobacco, coffee, and other commodities. The officer prisoners were those who either refused to live on parole or broke the parole rules. They engaged in theatricals, music, and art, funded by money sent to them by their families in France and lived the life of gentlemen by comparison with the men. The Americans were altogether of a different disposition, being unruly and defiant, although a number of them, like the French, volunteered for paid work (slave labour was forbidden) building Princetown Church and the Parsonage.

About 1250 Frenchmen died at Dartmoor prison, nearly 500 of them during the first year (victims of a particularly virulent measles epidemic), the rest from

The American Memorial
(Author's photo)

typhoid and other diseases, some who committed suicide, some killed in duels, and others were shot trying to escape. The Americans suffered around 260 fatalities, most of them dying when there was an outbreak of smallpox in 1814. All the dead were buried in shallow pits outside the prison walls in the area which is now part of the prison farm. In 1865, by which time Dartmoor had been converted to a convict prison, the ground was scattered with their bones which had surfaced due to erosion and the activities of animals. They were collected and divided by order of the Governor and interred in two mass graves surmounted by obelisks each of which was inscribed with the words: *Dulce et Decorum est pro Patria mori* (It is Sweet and Honourable to die for one's Country). The graves are situated in two separate areas at the rear of the prison.

When the wars ended the prisoners and their Military guards went home, leaving the prison in the hands of caretakers for the next 34 years. For a short time it was let to the British Naphtha Company who worked the peat bogs and constructed a tramway to transport the peat to the prison where retort furnaces had been installed for extracting the gas and oils (the track can still be traced over the moor below Fice's Well). Meanwhile the transportation of criminals was ending and another way of dealing with them had to be found. The solution was to establish penal institutions where convicted men would work on projects similar to that performed in the Colonies and Dartmoor was one of the locations chosen.

In September 1850 one of the old prison blocks was converted for the confinement of convicts, which required the provision of separate cells. The concrete floors were removed in order to construct iron cells, arranged back to back with landings between them and the outside walls for the warders to patrol. The first inmates lived in perpetual gloom with candles for lighting after dark.

The fit ones among them were put to work farming and quarrying. There was no recreation for them or the warders and the Silent Rule (no talking, whispering, or communication of any kind) was rigorously enforced. The convicts working outside the prison were guarded by units of the British Army, to be superseded later by the Civil Guard, a body of armed men comprised mainly of old soldiers. Prisoners laboured 'under the gun' for the next 100 years, during which time several were killed or maimed when guards opened fire on runaways. There was never a treadwheel at Dartmoor, nor were executions carried out there, but in common with other establishments punishments were severe: flogging with the 'cat o' nine tails' or the birch, for serious offences; restricted diet (three days on bread and water only); the wearing of heavy chains, canvas suits, and being placed in solitary confinement, are examples of how discipline was kept. Flogging, restricted diet, and armed guards for outside work parties were the norm until the 1950s and beyond.

The prison has changed dramatically since those early times. Four of the original blocks were demolished in the late 1800s and new granite buildings took their place. They have held some of the worst rogues and criminals this country has ever known. Among them were the 'Titchbourne Claimant', whose fraudulent claim to a missing (presumed drowned in a shipwreck) aristocrat's

Dartmoor Prison's grim grey walls
Courtesy Mr B. Jones

inheritance resulted in the longest trial in British legal history; John George Haigh, dubbed 'the acid bath murderer' for killing a widow, after charming her into parting with her money and disposing of the body by dissolving it in a bath of sulphuric acid (he served time at Dartmoor for fraud before committing the murders for which he was found guilty and hanged); James Camb, a former ship's steward who was convicted of murdering the actress Gay Gibson on board the Union Castle liner 'Durban Castle' and dumping her body in the sea. It was the first murder conviction without a body being produced, and he was probably the first man to be reprieved after being sentenced to death just before hanging was temporarily, and later permanently abolished. Then there was the 'Mad Axeman', Frank Mitchell, whose story is the first to be told in this book. The Irish have featured in Dartmoor's past too, starting with members of the Fenian organisation in the 1860s and Mr. Eamon De Valera, future Prime Minister and President of the Republic of Ireland who was jailed for taking part in the Easter rising in Dublin in 1916, and served part of his sentence on the 'moor'; and in 1939 a number of IRA members were in custody. In 1917 the prison was given over to 1000 'Conscientious Objectors' who chose to go to prison rather than abandon their (mostly religious) principles by going to the war.

Dartmoor prison has been extensively modernised in recent years and inmates have electric lighting, central heating, and telephone contact with their families, a far cry from the days when a man practically lost all contact with the outside world for the duration of his sentence. Prisoners are treated more humanely now than ever before and the harsh conditions that gave Dartmoor its fearsome reputation no longer apply. In common with other establishments it has updated its facilities and plays its part in new initiatives aimed at helping offenders. There are some who say a prison sentence is 'easy', but to be deprived of liberty can be a devastating experience. A Dartmoor inmate lives and eats alone in his cell and the hours he spends working or training, taking exercise, and the two hours a day allocated for Association, are the only occasions when he has contact with his fellow men. When the key turns to lock him in his cell at 8.00pm he finds himself alone with his thoughts and his conscience, just like the convicts of old.

FRANK MITCHELL THE 'MAD AXEMAN'

There was never an escape from prison that caught the public's attention more than that of Frank Mitchell who disappeared from an outside work party in December 1966. It was a typical winter's day on Dartmoor, windy, cold and wet, when 'Big Frank' literally vanished. Stories about his eventual fate vary, but there can be no doubt he was assisted by London based criminals and was later murdered for reasons we can only speculate on.

Dartmoor prison officers remember him as a man who rejoiced in his enormous physical strength and took every opportunity to show it off. A gentle giant with the mind of a child, he would turn into a raging bull of a man in an instant if something upset him; yet in the main, he was a trouble free inmate providing he was constantly humoured and tactfully handled. His real name was Frank Ellis, but he was always known as and is remembered as Frank Samuel Mitchell, an alias. For a big man he wasn't tall, under 6ft., with very broad shoulders and a huge chest; 'stocky' would be an appropriate word to use in describing him. The newspapers dubbed him the 'Mad Axeman', but Frank was not 'mad' in the true sense of the word, and was not a murderer either. He was certainly a tough and highly dangerous individual who 'ruled the roost' unopposed over his fellow inmates. He arrived at Dartmoor with a fearsome reputation, not solely on account of the physical violence he was capable of, but also because during a previous term of imprisonment he was suspected of slashing another inmate with a 'chiv' (prison term for a home made knife). When he was allowed to join outside work parties, against the advice of experienced officers, several people living on or near the moor openly expressed fears for their safety. The late James Mildren, a well known and respected local journalist, was approached on at least two occasions by a lady who lived on the edge of the moor who was frightened and wanted reassurance. He raised the matter with the prison, but to no effect; yet when Mitchell went missing there was a national outcry and the Home Secretary faced a barrage of criticism over the decision to permit such a man to work outside the prison. To understand this we need to examine Mitchell's record:

He was born in Kennington in the Borough of Lambeth in 1929, and attended a special school for backward children. He became a delinquent at an early age and graduated to crime where his activities included housebreaking, office breaking, and ultimately robbery with violence, all of which earned him terms of imprisonment. He was friendly with the three Kray brothers and knew them well enough to correspond with them, and they with him, when he was in prison (he probably helped out now and then on 'The Firm', as they called themselves). He was an unruly, violent inmate, and in two recorded instances corporal punishment was administered.

Pentonville 1954. 15 strokes with the 'cat o' nine tails' for gross personal violence. He had assaulted three warders.

Hull Prison 1962. 15 strokes with the birch for attacking two warders.

He was a very dangerous individual who, because of his bad behaviour and uncontrollable tantrums, was sent to Rampton and later to Broadmoor. He escaped from both institutions and whilst on the run from Broadmoor robbed an elderly couple in their home after threatening them with an axe, thus earning his title 'The Mad Axeman'. In 1958, at Berkshire Assizes, he was sentenced to life imprisonment for robbery with violence with no fixed date for his release.

At Dartmoor, his last prison, stories about Frank Mitchell are numerous and impressive. One retired prison officer who knew him well said: "He was a giant of a man, a fitness fanatic who was always exercising in his cell or at work. He would pick up iron bars, boulders, in fact anything to hand and lift them above his head. On one occasion an inmate, a heavily-built man, was injured in the quarry and I was about to send for a stretcher when Mitchell intervened. 'No need for that Guv' he said, 'I'll carry him for you.' 'You will never do it' I told him — but he did. I helped get the casualty on his shoulders and he carried him non-stop all the way to the prison and into the hospital, a distance of half a mile or more." Another officer recalls how Mitchell once lifted two officers at once in a 'bear hug', one under each arm. "It was his idea of being playful, but his regular minders kept out of his way because he'd broken an officer's bones doing that in another prison — he didn't know his own strength." Yet another ex-prison employee tells how he got hold of the prison Governor, Mr. Denis Malone, and lifted him in the air. "Come on Frank, put me down there's a good chap." he said, and he was set down unharmed. Tales about

Frank carrying a 3cwt. sack of coire from the stores to the mat making shop, and lifting the rear of a Triumph Vitesse police car with two officers inside and turning it 180 degrees, are enshrined in Dartmoor's history.

It appears the only way to manage Mitchell was to humour him, and this helps explain why he was allowed a degree of freedom and tolerance not permitted to other inmates. He sort of tagged along on the work parties with no intention of working, carrying an axe on his ample shoulders, thus perpetuating the 'Axeman' title he bore. Mr. Malone, who was a very fair-minded Governor, considered it was wrong for him to be detained indefinitely and tried to get him a release date from the Home Secretary. Whether or not Mitchell knew about this is uncertain, but it turned out it was his prime motive for escaping and he (Mitchell) sought to bring it to the public's attention, and the Home Secretary's, in letters he wrote to two national newspapers whilst in hiding after his escape. Ironically, the Home Secretary, under questioning in the Commons, stated Mitchell's case was already under review with the intention of fixing a date for his release. It was too late, the bird had flown.

One Sunday in December 1966 a large grey Rover car was seen in the Two Bridges area by the Vicar of Princetown, the late Rev. Courtney Johns and his wife. On a winter's day in the 1960s such a sight was rare, and the Vicar decided to report what he'd seen to the police. The same car had called at the Forest Inn at Hexworthy, not far from Princetown, and three very well dressed men with London accents had lunch there. They were visiting an acquaintance at Dartmoor prison, they told the landlord. Was that acquaintance Frank Mitchell, and was the purpose of their visit to formulate an escape plan? It seems more than likely because just a couple of weeks later their car was again spotted on the moor the day before the 'Big Escape' took place.

Mitchell's work party was engaged in erecting fences at Bagga Tor, about eight miles from the prison. They were taken there each morning by minibus and collected in the afternoon to be returned to the prison. Lunch was taken in a hut close by, and prepared by one of the prisoners from supplies they brought with them. Men who were selected for the 'Honour Parties', as they were called then, were generally those with only a short time left to serve and who had good behaviour records (all the more remarkable Mitchell was included). As only one officer was in charge, and because some prisoners necessarily worked beyond his field of vision, it would have been easy for any one of them to slip away unobserved. Mitchell it seems, was in the habit of doing just that, and when the story of his escape appeared in the newspapers, together with his photograph, there were several local people who recognised him as a regular visitor to their

Constable (later Superintendent) D. Roper, the Princetown "Bobby", making enquiries. Courtesy Simon Dell M.B.E.

village pubs — including some landlords. On one occasion he took a taxi ride to Tavistock and bought a budgerigar. Statements confirming these events were made on oath at the subsequent trial of the three Kray brothers, together with some of their associates, on charges of aiding Mitchell to escape, harbouring him, and murdering him. An astonished Judge declared: "It all sounds cloud cuckoo to me!", a sentiment he shared with an equally astonished British public.

On the afternoon of Monday 12 December 1966 the weather was atrocious on Dartmoor and Mitchell's party took shelter in their hut. Frank left the hut on a pretext and did not reappear. There was no radio communication with the prison in those days, and when he failed to turn up for the journey back, the officer in charge raised the alarm by telephoning from a public call box in Peter Tavy, the nearest village. The Princetown resident policeman, Constable D. Roper, was at Postbridge on an enquiry when the prison rang to say Frank Mitchell was reported missing from a work party, and it was his wife, Rosemary, who took the call. "I was frightened and locked all the doors and windows," she told the author. "It was the only time during our posting to Princetown I was ever scared, but I was alone in the house with darkness coming on, and two young children to care for. I was quite apprehensive." Mrs. Roper, like all Princetown residents, knew that escaped prisoners always headed away from the town, but who could say what a 'mad axeman' might do? She was not the only person to be alarmed by Mitchell's escape. A man living with his wife in Mount Tavy Road on the outskirts of Tavistock, later confessed to keeping a gun under the bed after hearing the news.

One of the biggest manhunts ever mounted for an escaped Dartmoor prisoner was then organised. The police set up road blocks and officers with tracker dogs searched moorland farms, outhouses, cattle sheds and barns. They were assisted in scouring the moors and commons by soldiers of the Wessex Brigade, Royal Marine Commandos from 41 Commando, Bickleigh, and men of the Argyll and Sutherland Highlanders from Seaton Barracks, Crownhill. Prison officers were allocated to search parties looking for the man the Press called 'the most dangerous criminal in England' and a Royal Air Force helicopter from Chivenor, North Devon, was called in to help (the police force did not yet have one).

They were still looking for Mitchell at Christmas. On 29 December a retired prison officer who had known him when he was serving at Broadmoor made a personal appeal to him on nationwide television to give himself up. "Frank," he said, "you've made your point, and the sooner you give yourself up the better your case will be... if you wish to approach me I will do all I can to assist you and convey you to the authorities." He went on to say he thought Mitchell could be trusted in certain circumstances, but he objected to uniformed authority — it was a 'red rag' to him. It was a wasted effort because by then Frank Mitchell was dead, murdered by persons unknown; in any case, we now know he was off the moor and on the road to London before he was even reported missing.

On Sunday 11 December, the day before the escape, the big Rover car turned up again at the Forest Inn at Hexworthy and three muscular, smartly dressed men had breakfast. In the afternoon two of them were admitted as visitors to Dartmoor prison, using what were later found to be false names. That evening a garage attendant in Tavistock spoke to them on the forecourt when they asked for a map of the area. When they were told there was not one available they drove off after receiving directions on how to get to Peter Tavy, a village near Bagga Tor where Mitchell's party was working. It seems certain they picked up Frank Mitchell by arrangement the next day and by nightfall he was installed in a flat in East Ham, London. When prison clothing with his prison number stamped on it was found a day or two later in a lay-by at Tedburn St. Mary, between Okehampton and Exeter on the old main A30 road leading out of the county, the search was extended to the London area. Armed police visited the homes of known criminals who might have been harbouring him, but without success.

Meanwhile, an embarrassed Home Secretary and a new Dartmoor prison

Governor (Mr. Malone had retired to New Zealand) were having to explain several anomalies concerning one of the most sensational episodes in the entire history of the prison. What was a man like Mitchell doing in Dartmoor in the first place? Shouldn't he have been sent back to Broadmoor or similar institution? With a history of violence, previous escapes, and an indefinite period still to serve, why was he permitted to join an outside work party? Why was the advice of senior prison officers not to allow Mitchell outside the prison ignored? These are some of the questions which were asked in the House of Commons and by Mr. Michael Heseltine, M.P. for Tavistock. As a result, the Committee of Enquiry, under Lord Louis Mountbatten, which had been set up to enquire into the circumstances surrounding the escape of the convicted spy, George Blake, from Wormwood Scrubs in October 1966, was given the additional task of investigating recent events at Dartmoor. A high security fence, floodlighting, the formation of a prison dog section, and (to the prison officers' delight) a radio communication system were among the Enquiry's recommendations, all of which were implemented.

At the trial of the Kray brothers it was alleged 'Big Frank' was killed on 23 December after only 11 days of 'freedom' cooped up in the London flat. It was never established why or who did it; no-one was convicted of his murder, and his body was never found. Ronald Kray, in his book 'My Story' (Pan Books) claims he knows who killed Mitchell and names an associate, Billy Exley, who he says was paid to take him out of the country with the help of three Greeks and that they murdered him instead. It was Exley who later tipped off the police it was the Krays who did it, and gave evidence for the prosecution at their trial. Whoever was responsible, what did the murderers do with the body? The story is told within the Prison Service that several prisoners, whilst being transferred from one prison to another, have pointed out to their escorts the same concrete pillar supporting a motorway bridge which, they say, is where Mitchell's corpse was disposed of in a mix of concrete. Another chilling account alleges his killers studied the funeral notices in the newspapers and put his body in a ready dug grave late at night, under the lining. The legal occupant was afterwards interred on top and Frank Mitchell was lost to the world for ever.

Two prison Chaplains who made assessments of Mitchell in prison have the last word. One of them strikes an optimistic note after finding him reading poetry in his cell: "This man has a fund of fearlessness and courage which could, in other circumstances, have made him a very useful citizen." The second is prophetic and nearer the truth one feels: "A tough-seeming, but weak, impressionable young man, fond of posing as the toughest of the boys ... *there seems almost no hope for his future.*" (Author's italics).

THE AMERICAN'S MASTER PLAN

In April 1813 the French prisoners at Dartmoor were joined by 250 Americans, mostly sailors captured during the War of 1812 (Britain was fighting two wars at this time). When the war with Napoleon ended in April 1814, the French were repatriated, and all American POWs in England were transferred to Dartmoor (except the officers who were on Parole). They lost no time in planning to escape, and there are several recorded instances where, like the French, they either fooled or bribed the guards or simply made a run for it. The following is an account of a carefully planned, co-ordinated, effort that would have had spectacular results had it succeeded.

In August 1814 they formulated a master escape plan to tunnel their way out under the prison walls. This was to be the most ambitious attempt at a mass breakout ever devised by prisoners on the 'moor.' They had the place to themselves now the French had gone. They had previously been confined to the north side of the compound (see diagram); now they were permitted to make use of Number Six block to ease the congestion, and as more prisoners arrived,

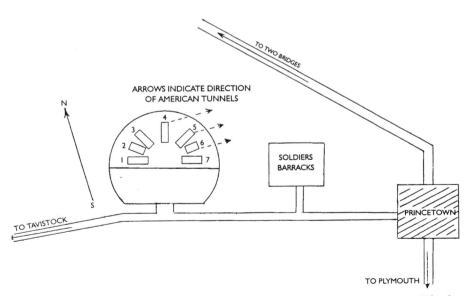

Dartmoor Prison 1812. Diagram showing arrangement of Prisoners' Blocks. The Americans were aiming for the Two Bridges Road.

they too went to Number Six. This is where the digging began.

Secrecy was vital of course. Bibles were procured and every man involved swore on oath not to reveal by word or sign what was going on; the penalty for treachery was to be death by hanging, a sentence they themselves would carry out. The overcrowding in Number Four block (which was inside a separate walled-off area) was to be eased by moving men to Number Six, so it was decided to extend the plan to include tunnelling from Number Four as well. Then the unoccupied Number Five block was included in the plan. With prisoners passing the entrance all day it was easy for some to slip inside and start work there; thus there were three tunnels being excavated at once, and their feeling was that should any one tunnel be discovered the chances were at least one would remain undetected.

In 'A Prisoner's Memoires', a book written by an American prisoner called Charles Andrews, published in America after the war, they claim to have sunk shafts 20ft. deep before digging outwards horizontally in an easterly direction. They found the subterranean soil to be light and relatively free of stones, so progress was good. The entrances were very narrow but underground the holes were wide enough for four men to work abreast, and they rigged lamps in a way that induced a circulation of air, stale air being expelled as fresh air entered. The biggest problem was disposing of the excavated material. At first pocketfuls of earth were scattered over the yards, but a more effective way had to be found if progress was to be maintained. The bulk of the dirt was thrown into the fast flowing foul water outlets and an ingenious method was devised for getting rid of the remainder. The prisons were built of roughly dressed 'moor stone' which left large crevices in the walls. The Americans mixed the sandy soil they brought up into a rough mortar and filled in the cracks, disguising their work by whitewashing over it. The prison officials afterwards expressed amazement at the amount of material that must have been dug out and never understood how it was disposed of. By the end of August they had progressed over 60ft. in each tunnel. Then disaster struck when on 2 September, the authorities began a search of Numbers Five and Six blocks. They found one of the entrances, but only after tapping the floors with crowbars, so cleverly was it concealed. All of the prisoners were sent back to occupy Numbers One, Two and Three blocks and the tunnel was sealed off with stones. (In 1881, during excavations to lay the foundations for a new convict prison, the tunnel was uncovered and found to be 14ft. deep, not 20ft. as the Americans had claimed. An enterprising convict who later occupied a cell directly over the tunnel tried to escape by digging down into it, only to find it was still full of stones.) Had they been betrayed? An enquiry was held amongst themselves and several prisoners were interrogated on suspicion of turning traitor, but the evidence was inconclusive and it was supposed that careless talk had alerted the authorities. Number Four prison block was not searched and work recommenced there at once. In September more prisoners began arriving and Numbers Five, Six and Seven blocks had to be made available again to accommodate them. Excavations were immediately resumed and Number Six tunnel was reopened by men digging around the blockages to reach the old workings. The task was again co-ordinated with the intention of completing all three tunnels simultaneously, when hundreds of men would pass through them and make their way to the coast. The mass escape was planned for 10.00pm one stormy night, which would allow time for them to reach the Torbay area before daylight. The men were elated, working eagerly, and confident of success. Then there was a betrayal when one of their number approached the guards and went off with them, never to be seen again. It was thought he had been repatriated as a reward for his treachery. Once more every man was sent back to the north side of the prison, regardless of overcrowding, whilst repairs were made and the tunnels blocked up. The Americans were placed on two thirds rations for ten days, the remaining one third being retained to cover the cost of the work. It was devastating blow for them, and Andrews wrote "If the villain had been caught, they should scarcely have tried him but would have torn him to atoms before the life could have time to leave his traitorous body."

Until the very day of their release the 'Yankees' were bitter enemies, causing unrest and exasperating their captors to the extent one British officer openly proclaimed he would sooner deal with 10,000 Frenchmen than 4,000 American prisoners. Had their tunnels gone undetected many hundreds of them would have been at large and the prison officials would have had to face a problem of unprecedented magnitude — with a headache to match!

BLOODHOUNDS ON THE TRAIL.

On Friday 6 February 1931 Dartmoor prison warders and the residents of Princetown were alerted by the clanging of the huge bell suspended above the prison's main entrance. Two convicts had just escaped and the bell rang to summon off duty warders to join their colleagues in searching for them. It was 2.30pm and conditions could not have been worse: there was thick fog, drizzle, and an icy cold wind blowing.

The escapees were Michael Gaskin, 31, serving five years for false pretences and forgery, and John Mullins, a 28 year old in for housebreaking. They were old friends, having served together in France during World War 1 and had planned their escape over a five month period, a plan that called for fitness and speed. They worked in the stone sheds just inside the boundary wall, and they returned after the lunch break, the weather being favourable for their purpose, with a hidden length of rope to which was attached a hook to act as a grapnel. Suddenly, in perfect unison, they sprang into action, evading their guard (one report stated he was overpowered) and in less than a minute had secured the rope and climbed the vertical 24 ft. high wall to freedom.

It was the first escape from Dartmoor in three years, and as the two men ran off, completely hidden by the mist, warders dashed to prearranged check points, some in borrowed cars, others on motor cycles, in the hope they would contain them within an area that could be thoroughly searched afterwards. Several young men from Princetown followed too, hopeful of a chance to earn the £5 reward payable for apprehending them. Mounted warders on stout ponies headed for their posts on the moor to look, listen, and search for clues and it was the 'mounties' who discovered arrowed footprints on the banks of the Devonport Leat which flows past the prison towards the rear of the Tor Royal Estate. They also found a prison jacket in the leat itself, indicating the direction the convicts had taken. It was a clever move because instead of fleeing blindly over the open moor, the leat would lead them to Burrator Reservoir and the Meavy valley, leaving the warders hunting for them an impossible task with the mist persisting and darkness coming on.

Devon County Police were alerted and immediately roads throughout the county were put under observation in case the escapees stole a vehicle (both of them were known to be competent drivers). Incidentally, while all this was going on, actors at the Repertory Theatre in Devonport were rehearsing for a performance of John Galsworthy's play "Escape!", a tale of a Dartmoor prisoner's escape and subsequent recapture!

Saturday came and the rain poured down. The missing men had betrayed their whereabouts by the inevitable need to break into a house for a change of clothing and something to eat. 'Withermarsh', near Yelverton, the home of Mr. E.Redman, was their target, and they got what they wanted on Friday evening when Mr. Redman was away shopping. Besides stealing food the two men took a change of clothing which included a trilby hat and raincoat, items that were to prove crucial in putting the pursuing police and warders on their trail later. Meanwhile, with the thick mist still hampering the search, help came from a Miss Lowe of Minions, near Liskeard, who came forward with the loan of three bloodhounds, a gesture that was much appreciated at the time and was to be of enormous value in the hunt. Despite the wet ground, the hounds picked up the scent near the prison and successfully led the search parties to Mr. Redman's house and then to Gratton Bridge plantations where they found the prisoners' discarded uniforms. By this time it was dark and the hunt had to be called off.

The following (Sunday) morning, there was a breakthrough when Mullins was caught in an unexpected manner. He and Gasken had separated in the night, after calling at a house in Tamerton Foliot to ask for a drink. As it was nearly midnight, the occupier suspected who they might be, with the result the area was soon being combed by police, and when a late night bus came along with headlights blazing the two men scrambled over the hedge to right and left to avoid being seen. They were afraid to call to each other in case they were heard, so went their different ways in the dark. At daylight Mullins found shelter in a biscuit factory under construction in the Hartley district of Plymouth.

It was the relentless pouring rain and the action of a conscientious charge hand, Mr. W. Grainger of Corporation Road, that led to his recapture. He was concerned about the tools that were left on site, fearing they might get rusty, so he took the trouble to go and check on them and when he caught sight of Mullins he ordered him off the premises. When he showed a marked reluctance to go his suspicions were aroused because like everyone else he'd read the newspapers and knowing there were convicts on the run, he decided to walk casually away and get help. By coincidence, Mr. Grainger lived next door to a Plymouth City policeman, and asked a passer-by to go and fetch him, remaining in the vicinity himself to keep observation. When Constable Couch appeared a defiant Mullins said he'd 'fight for it', but it was a futile gesture. After 48 hours on the run, wet through, cold and hungry, he lacked the physical ability to match his fighting spirit and surrendered. "We didn't even handcuff him he was so subdued." said P.C. Couch afterwards.

Gasken was made of sterner stuff and remained at large for another two days. When an officer's briefcase was stolen from Crownhill Barracks he was the prime suspect. He had been stationed there in his army days and knew the place well, including Crownhill Fort with its maze of underground tunnels and passageways. Dozens of soldiers of the Wiltshire Regt. searched the fort but without success. A sentry had seen a man answering Gasken's description loitering near the barracks wearing a trilby hat and raincoat identical to those stolen from Yelverton. Now he had vanished into the dusk in heavy rain and mist. Because there was £10 in the missing briefcase, a watch was put on all railway stations in case he bought a train ticket to get clear of the county.

On Monday the hunt continued but of Gasken there was no sign. Police and Dartmoor warders had spent three days and nights watching roads and railways, tramping over moors and fields, following up reported sightings, restricted by mist, relentless rain, and penetrating cold winds. Now the warders were withdrawn in accordance with prison regulations, having been out three days, and the search was left to the police.

"Where is the second man?" the newspapers were asking. No-one would have guessed that Gasken, with breathtaking audacity, had spent almost all of Monday in the warmth and comfort of Laira (Plymouth) library, where he read the newspaper accounts about Mullins' recapture and the intensified hunt for him. He had even managed to sell a stolen pullover and bought two hot pasties and some tea on the proceeds. The crunch came when the library closed and he had to take to the streets; there was nowhere for him to go, no-one to turn to for help and he spent the night wandering about, ending up in the extensive railway sidings at Laira on Tuesday morning. There he was viewed with suspicion by railway workers who, although mistaking him for a plain clothes policeman at first, were alerted by another railwayman who found a discarded coat and torch after Gasken passed by. They summoned the police and were able to give them an accurate description of the wanted man. This was the lead the County police needed and men were drafted in from as far away as Totnes and Lifton, together with Miss Lowe's bloodhounds who were rushed to Laira to join them in helping Plymouth City police carry out the biggest manhunt ever mounted in the city, and the very first with hounds. A thorough, painstaking examination of every truck and hiding place in the yard was initiated, but without success. For Gasken the end came, as it did for Mullins, in an unexpected way.

He had already left the sidings and was strolling along Jinkins Avenue in nearby Lipson, having left the jacket and torch with the intention of misleading his pursuers. Unaware of the bloodhounds tracking him, and full of confidence, he ignored two policemen on the opposite side of the road and passed the time of day with two road workers. It was a mistake. One of them, Mr. W.Best, noted the flannel trousers tucked into Wellington boots and thought it strange attire for town wear; then he noticed the stranger had a mole on his cheek and realised he could be the escaped convict he'd read about in the newspapers. "I gave Jack Algar (his colleague) the wink" he said afterwards, "and he slipped across to the Sergeant." The game was up. Sgt. Palmer and Constable Maddock detained the suspect and sent for their supervisor Det. Insp. Lucas. "Hello Gasken," he said, "you're coming with me, you're missing from your home at Dartmoor." "My name is Brooks — you're making a big mistake. You'll be sorry for this!" Gasken blustered. He denied his identity right up to the moment he entered Plymouth Central Police Station for further questioning, then he cracked and admitted everything, but denied he had stolen the briefcase with the £10 inside. "If I had that kind of money I'd be dressed like an Eton boy." he declared. Any doubts about how the episode would have otherwise ended were dispelled when it was learned the party with the bloodhounds came panting up Jinkins Avenue within minutes of his arrest, hot on his trail.

Gasken was treated very kindly as he waited for an escort back to Dartmoor. Beef sandwiches, tea and cigarettes were freely given as he joked with his captors about his experiences. His face and hands were badly scratched and he was ravenously hungry; but otherwise he was in surprisingly good shape after spending days being hunted across country in atrocious weather with little food and cat-napping under hedgerows . Only later did the full effects of his escapade take their toll. Mullins was already in the prison hospital with a severe chill and Gasken joined him on his return in a serious condition, having developed pneumonia. He had learned a hard lesson, admitting to the police after his recapture "I didn't know what Dartmoor was like — I'll never try it again."

KEYS

One day in March 1862 a Dartmoor warder on patrol saw a prisoner called Anderson look out from the doorway of his cell. The warder's astonishment could only have been matched by Anderson's dismay. After taking him away to be locked up again the warders carried out a search of his cell and found a skeleton key that had been painstakingly made by an unlucky escapee who happened to pick the wrong moment to look and see if the coast was clear. Six years previously, on 25 August 1856, it was a warder who was unlucky. Convict James Lake had made a duplicate cell key out of bone salvaged from his meat ration. He fitted it to a piece of stick, put his arm through the ventilation slot adjacent to the door of his iron cell, and managed to insert it into the lock outside. After getting out of his cell he used the key again to liberate another man and together they overpowered the night warder, but their escape attempt was foiled when, during the struggle, the warder's cries alerted his colleagues who were quickly on the scene to apprehend the two convicts and lock them up once more.

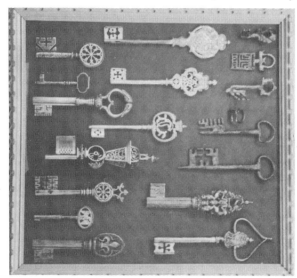

Examples of old gaol keys (various).
Courtesy of Dartmoor Prison Museum.

Prisoners have been making duplicate keys ever since the convict prison opened and Dartmoor prison's museum has a collection of them, most of which were confiscated during routine cell searches. The materials used range from wood and bone to plastic and odd scraps of metal. One was fashioned from a toothbrush handle and is still recognisable as such. Many years ago a key was reportedly discovered made from a stiff piece of cardboard. "Of what use is a key made of cardboard?" I hear you ask. Answer: an inmate trying to escape only needs to use it once!

There are, as you might expect, experts among the prison population to whom most locks present no barrier, which is why prison locks are specially manufactured and guaranteed to be unique in a ratio of several thousand to one. All the same, every lock requires a key and every prisoner is able to observe them several times each day when prison officers lock and unlock cell doors, entrance gates etc. One man, new to the job, was fumbling with lock and key when a passing inmate cheerfully called "You've got the wrong key Guv, you want that one!" pointing to another on the bunch.

Would you believe an inmate could make a key out of an odd bit of metal that perfectly matches a prison key, and to a pattern committed to memory, simply by seeing that key in use? It has happened more than once. During training sessions the story is told about a certain prison Governor who habitually waved a key at prisoners when admonishing them. The pattern was memorised and a duplicate was made (and later found). Strict precautions are taken when disposing of unwanted or worn-out keys. At Dartmoor, the pattern is first destroyed by burning with acetylene torches, after which the shanks are buried in concrete to prevent them falling into the wrong hands. The loss of a key or discovery of a duplicate is an extremely serious matter because every lock that key fits has to be changed. In recent years other prisons have had to change hundreds of locks, once for example, when the imprint of a key was discovered in a piece of pastry hidden in the kitchens, and on another occasion because a duplicate key was found in a cell. On 10 March 1998 the Daily Mail reported an incident at Wakefield Prison, Yorkshire, when an inmate was apprehended letting himself back *in* with a skeleton key. He had unlocked three doors and a gate in the security fence, and it was thought he was making a 'dummy run' in preparation for a planned escape when associates would pick him up. In the same year a cell key was lost at Dartmoor and locks had to be changed.

Modern cells have solid metal doors (although there are still a small number of old style wooden ones at Dartmoor) without a handle or locking mechanism on the inside, so escaping from a cell is a rare occurrence. The risk arises when inmates leave their cells to go to exercise or to work. On Boxing Day 1966 five Dartmoor prisoners ganged up on their two supervising officers in the gymnasium, tied them up, and stole their keys in order to escape. In his book 'The Story of Dartmoor Prison' former Governor Mr. Basil Thomson relates how a warder lost a key in April 1860. A series of escape attempts with a reproduction key took place, and several more were later discovered. 'The trail of the lost key may be traced in the prison records for more than ten years' he wrote. Imagine how often it must have been copied and how many ounces of precious tobacco changed hands among inmates anxious to gain possession of it.

AM I SEEING THINGS?

Imagine a winter's day on Dartmoor when it is snowing and there's an inmate missing from the prison. Two policemen in a Land Rover were on their way to Princetown as part of a search team when they spotted a car stuck on 'Halifax Corner', a notorious 'S' bend on the hill above Merrivale on the Tavistock road west of Princetown. When they got closer they gaped at what they saw, for at the rear of the car, pushing with all his might, was a figure in convict clothes, complete with forage cap and the famous black arrow markings! The driver looked hopefully at the Land Rover as it went by. "Do you see what I see? We'd better have a look." said one of the officers to his colleague. They stopped and one of them walked back to the car. The chap who was doing the pushing wore a worried frown as the policeman looked him over before addressing the driver. "May I ask who you are and where you are going and," with a grim look at the arrow-suited figure, "who this is?" "It's alright officer, I'm .... a Dartmoor Prison officer, and this is my son — he's on his way home from his school's fancy dress party." "I see," said the policeman, taking a step towards the 'convict', who was edging away, "you look as if you could do with some help!" he said cheerily. The three of them laughed as a uniformed officer of the Devon and Cornwall Constabulary took his place beside a uniformed 'convict', and helped a Prison Officer out of a tight corner.

FATHER FINNEGAN'S CAR

It was a blue Clyno two-seater, a 1923 model and the very first of its kind, that escaped convict George Whitehead stole and made history by using it to get away from Dartmoor prison, the first escape ever by car from the 'moor'.

It happened on Sunday 15 April 1928 when the prison was obscured by a mist so thick visibility was down to fifteen yards. Whitehead, who was a dangerous 28-year-old serving a seven year sentence for shop breaking, garage breaking, and shooting with intent, had formulated a meticulous plan of escape. The prison regime then was quite different to what it is today; for example, attendance at the prison chapel for a short service every morning before starting work was compulsory. On Sundays there was an hour long service from which Whitehead was exempt because he had the job of bath house attendant (all convicts bathed once a week in a communal bath house on a rota basis) and during Sunday services, which were held between 10.30am and 11.30am he was locked in the bath house to complete his cleaning duties. On this occasion, when the warders returned to collect him, they found the place empty! He had

1926 Clyno 11h.p. 2-seater.
Photo reproduced with the permission of the National Motor Museum, Beaulieu, Hants

somehow managed to break out (exactly how was never revealed) and cross the empty prison yards unobserved, because of the mist, to the Blacksmith shop. Within minutes he had broken in and stolen two ladders which he joined together and used to get over the prison wall and down the other side. He then dumped the ladders in the old French cemetery at the rear of the prison in order to confuse his pursuers, and doubled back to the Princetown–Rundlestone road, which he crossed to take cover in the (then) thickly wooded hillside opposite.

His next move was bold in the extreme, because instead of making for the open moor, away from Princetown, he turned towards the town, hastening through the trees within yards of Dartmoor prison's main entrance. His objective was the home of Father Finnegan, the prison's Roman Catholic priest, whose house was the very first one he would come to on the outskirts of the town. Immediately in front of the house was a detached garage containing his cherished Clyno car. From the hillside Whitehead was able to step onto the garage roof, and after removing several roof tiles, lowered himself between the support girders to within. It was a particularly audacious undertaking because his point of entry was in full view of the house and the road, even in the mist, and at any moment a passing motorist or pedestrian might have spotted him. Furthermore, nearly every prison warder going to and from the prison passed that very spot, their quarters being close to hand. Whitehead even took his time over stealing the car, pausing to top up the petrol tank and putting a spare can of petrol on board. He also took a waterproof overcoat to wear over his prison clothes. Then he started the car, flung open the garage doors, and drove boldly down Princetown's main street to the junction opposite the 'Plume of Feathers' Inn. Standing there was the town's resident policeman. The convict ignored him, spun the steering wheel, and sped away towards Two Bridges, leaving in his wake a puzzled Constable who, although he was unable to see who was driving, knew the vehicle and its owner and had his arm half raised in a salute. The escapee was on his way over the moors in the direction of Ashburton before the warders at the prison missed him.

The circumstances which enabled Whitehead to escape with such ruthless efficiency are worth relating. Firstly, he was a skilled motor mechanic, so taking and driving away a strange car was no problem for him; secondly, he had served a previous term of imprisonment at Dartmoor, during which he had worked outside the prison and thereby 'knew the lay of the land'; thirdly, between sentences he was employed as a charabanc driver taking parties of visitors from Torquay on outings to Princetown, so the roads were familiar to him. Finally, he obviously knew exactly where Father Finnegan's car was and that he would be conducting Mass at the time of his escape. The prison was quick to respond once his disappearance became known, so quick in fact the alarm was never raised. Whitehead's description was communicated to the police as warders rushed to man cars and motor cycles to go in pursuit of him. When the police learned about the stolen car, not only were all roads leading out of Devon put under observation, but it was decided to concentrate the search in the Totnes–Torquay area which he knew so well. Meanwhile, prison warders were racing after him along the mist shrouded roads as fast as they dared and, it was afterwards ascertained, were hot on his trail when unfortunately their vehicle broke down. The fugitive speeding ahead of them was in fact heading for Torbay via Ashburton, Buckfastleigh and Totnes as predicted.

A strong police presence had been established at Totnes on the assumption this would be his objective and this was confirmed in dramatic fashion when two policemen, stationed at a road junction on the approach to the town, saw the wanted man driving towards them very fast. They were impressed by the speed and skill with which he reacted. Skidding to a halt within 70 yards of where they were, he reversed several yards and accelerated away in another direction. Whitehead knew the hunt for him would intensify now he'd been seen and that the net would soon close on him, which is why he took a chance by turning into a country lane leading across the Dartington Hall Estate. Here his luck ran out. Prison warders picked up the trail by following tyre marks up the lane and discovered the Clyno stuck up to its axles in mud with the engine still warm. Their quarry had fled, leaving footprints leading towards the woods surrounding the estate. A frantic car chase now turned into a manhunt as warders, police, and civilian volunteers began combing the area, but because the light was fading (it was now late afternoon) and it was raining heavily, the search was called off until daylight. Meanwhile, every road, railway and river crossing was watched by the police and the entire County of Devon was kept on full alert in case Whitehead stole another car — which is exactly what he did.

By now he must have been very tired, hungry and cold after ten hours on the run, yet he retained a high degree of resourcefulness despite the teeming rain that fell. Aware that the River Dart was between him and Torbay, and that he was effectively 'cornered', he managed to locate the river bank in the dark and was lucky enough to find a rowing boat which had been left for the night by some workmen, and used it to cross over. As the police waited patiently for the dawn before resuming their search, he was miles away, roaming the streets of Paignton looking for another car to steal. In George Street he found one, after forcing an entry into no less than four lockup garages, two of which contained cars under repair, and the third held a vehicle he couldn't start. In the fourth one he found a brand new Morris Oxford saloon which he drove away with ease.

A careless move by Whitehead plus the fact he'd been at liberty for more than fourteen hours without food or rest, and an unforeseen problem with the second stolen car, were the factors that led to his recapture. In the early hours of Monday morning he broke into a cafe at Meadfoot Beach in Torquay and feasted on biscuits, chocolate and milk. In his usual calm manner he loaded the car with a stock of these things for future consumption, but instead of driving away he made an incredible error of judgement, probably through sheer fatigue, and parked the car on Torquay's famous Marine Parade. There, without any attempt at concealment, he got in the back and went to sleep! A passer-by thought the sight of a roughly clad man sleeping in the back of a posh new car on the sea front at 6.00am on a Monday morning so strange he reported it to the police. Soon search parties were scouring the streets looking for Whitehead, for they realised at once who the sleeping man might be, and road blocks were set up to seal him in.

The convict had yet another stroke of good fortune however by waking up within minutes of going to sleep, and realising his predicament, made a run for it in the car, using his intimate knowledge of the town to elude the police. Another realisation quickly dawned on him when the Morris Oxford failed to deliver a turn of speed at a time when he needed it most. This was because all new Morris cars at that time were fitted with a speed regulator at the factory which prevented them being driven at more than 30 m.p.h. on the level until its first 500 mile service. The device was a simple rubber washer fitted in the carburettor and Whitehead obviously recognised the problem for what it was by turning into a quiet lane leading to Milbur Down where he thought it would be safe to stop and remove it. He hadn't noticed another special feature on the car though, namely the corded tyres which had a distinctive pattern and left an unmistakable track on the road (and there were plenty of them after the previous night of heavy rain). Two Torquay detectives who had been assigned to the search had taken note of the pattern and recognised them at once when they came across them. They then displayed exceptional patience by following them, and by a process of elimination when the track ran out on the dry patches of road, eventually traced the escapee to the lane where he was.

Whitehead was leaning over the engine, intent on his task, as the two men stalked him on foot, quietly and unobserved. At the last moment they were seen and their man bolted with the younger of the two detectives in pursuit. He had a revolver but he didn't need it. Lack of food and warmth had taken their toll and the convict stopped suddenly with the words: "It's all right, I'll come quietly." and he did, having been hunted for twenty four hours without rest. An outstanding feat of daring had come to naught. The Morris Oxford was returned to its rightful owner, a local dentist, who had only driven the car once since taking delivery of it and was naturally delighted to get it back undamaged. His wife greeted the news with a nod of her head towards their lockup garage. "We really must get that number changed now." she said. It was number thirteen.

THE FOLLOWING INSTRUCTIONS ARE ISSUED FOR THE GUIDANCE OF OFFICERS IN THE USE OF FIREARMS.
— 29th May 1935 —
ESCAPE OR ATTEMPTED ESCAPE.

1. In case of absolute necessity it is lawful to fire at a **Felon** but not at a **Misdemeanant** if an escape cannot otherwise be prevented.

2. If it becomes necessary to shoot, the first shot should be aimed well above the escaping convict, and if a second shot is required it should be aimed low so as to avoid the danger of wounding a vital part

MUTINY OR VIOLENCE.

1. If two or more convicts combine to escape or perform any act of mutiny or violence which is the legal duty of an officer to prevent, and if force is used or threatened by such convicts in resisting the officers in the execution of their duty, and there are reasonable grounds to suppose that the officers may be by such force overpowered or suffer bodily harm, then it is justifiable to use firearms if the force used or threatened by such convicts could not be resisted by other means.

2. If in any circumstances a convict gives an officer reasonable grounds for believing himself to be in peril of his life or bodily harm, the officer is entitled to use firearms if he cannot protect himself by other means.

3. Except in the case of absolute necessity a **Warning** should always be given before firearms are used, and as far as possible aim should always be taken to avoid wounding a vital part.

GOVERNOR

H.M. PRISON

DARTMOOR

Reproduced courtesy of Dartmoor Prison Museum.

VIOLENCE, GLAMOUR AND PUNISHMENTS

Prison escapes have in the past often been regarded as some kind of sporting event by members of the public who frequently gave recaptured prisoners an ovation similar to that directed at many television and 'pop' idols today. An extreme case was that of two escaped convicts who were cornered at South Tawton, near Okehampton, in 1851. A farmer and his son assisted the local Constable in capturing them and were badly injured in the struggle, the farmer being severely kicked and beaten. The Constable suffered head injuries after being hit with a stone tied in a handkerchief. All three men then had to fight off the populace, who sided with the runaways and plied them with tobacco and beer! One of the convicts was quite drunk when he was finally secured. Dartmoor prison's evil reputation was then in the making, which probably accounted for the South Tawton inhabitants sympathising with the fugitives.

The Rev. Clifford Rickards in 'A Prison Chaplain on Dartmoor' tells how several prisoners got away from a farm party near the prison, only to be recaptured almost at once. They were marched back through Princetown to the prison. Shouts of "They've got them!" and "Here they come." attracted the Reverend into the street in time to see a huge crowd of residents and visitors surrounding a group of warders escorting the escapees back to jail. Loud cheering and shouts of encouragement rang out, to the delight of the prisoners 'who laughed back at them and appeared to be having the time of their lives'. Rev. Rickards then relates another side of the story: further up the street a group of anxious women had gathered, all of them warder's wives. "It's no laughing matter for us," they said, "it's our husbands who will be made to suffer when the enquiry is made." And so it was: the warders, who were invariably held responsible for escapes, were fined or demoted for neglect of duty.

A similar, but less 'glamorous' episode, took place in 1879, and the excitement of the chase, together with the subsequent treatment of the recaptured men, was vividly portrayed by a convict who was present at the scene. He described the event in a letter smuggled out of Dartmoor to a prison acquaintance who had completed his sentence * . The instigator of the escape attempt was a prisoner named Morgan who had run away once before, and was obviously an 'opportunist' hell-bent on making a getaway.

The day's work was done and the farm party had stacked their rakes, forks, and tools before going to collect their hats and coats, which had been left beside

---

* Taken from "Convict Life" by 'Ticket of Leave Man' (Wyman & Sons 1879).

a hedge some distance away. "Now's our chance!" cried Morgan, and eight men disappeared over the hedge in a trice, 'leaving their guards open mouthed and decidedly off their guard. But of their escape there was no fear' the letter said, 'thirty or forty Devonshire labourers had heard the alarm whistle and the signal gun. They were soon joined by others and in strong parties started in pursuit. I think I may safely say that for the reward for each capture there will be at least half a dozen claimants'.

Meanwhile, the rest of the party were marched back to the prison, passing on the way 'an excited, pale faced youth, flourishing a double barrelled shotgun in a most alarming manner, exclaiming "Which way have they gone. Who will I shoot?" He has been the butt of a good many jokes since; for it was discovered when the time came to shoot he had left his ammunition pouch at his quarters!'

It being a perfectly clear evening with visibility of at least twenty miles, the fugitives were quickly rounded up. 'Last Friday', the letter went on, 'Director Morrish came down to Dartmoor redolent with the odour of Whitehall, and armed with all the majesty of a Supreme Judge. Five of the men received two dozen each with the 'cat' and the other three were birched. I saw the runaways this morning in their yellow dresses, they are breaking stones'. As for the warders, the account concludes: 'This morning the Governor received from Parliament-street the decision of the Directors as to the punishment of the officers who were in charge. They are each fined ten shillings' (ten shillings = 50p today. A warder's annual salary was less than £100 then) 'and reduced to Probation Class for three months, so their pay will be reduced for that period.'

The narrative closes on a touching note: 'And now our old friend .... will have to curtail the number of his visits to the Spotted Dog.'

JENNINGS' TAXI

One of the most daring escapes in Dartmoor's history occurred when three inmates stole an oil tanker and used it as a battering ram to smash their way out of the prison. The morning of Monday 24 June 1963 started quietly enough. At 9.00am a ten ton tanker lorry arrived to make a delivery of fuel oil to the boiler house, which is situated in the lower half of the prison's circular enclosure. Inmates on their way to exercise at 9.15am must have noticed its arrival and departure many times, and three of them, James Henry Jennings, 27, serving 15years for assault and robbery; Raymond Charles Matthews, 24, doing 10years for armed robbery; and Leslie Anthony Moore, 34, serving 5 years for office breaking and robbery; all had a particular interest in the proceedings that day. Getting out of prison was on their minds, and when they acted it was so swift and sudden everyone was taken by surprise.

The driver had finished unloading and was replacing the delivery hoses when the three prisoners broke away from the exercise yard and sprinted for the tanker, brushing the driver aside and hustling the escorting officer, who tried to restrain Moore, out of their way. They climbed into the cab and the engine roared as the tanker reversed out of the unloading bay, whilst the now stranded driver and prison officer companion did the only thing they could do in an effort to stop the escapees: they picked up all the loose stones they could find and threw them at the windscreen, shattering it. This failed to deter them though, and the driver watched helplessly as his vehicle headed for the main gate. A passing workman carrying cans of paint hurled them at the windows, breaking one of them as the lorry went by, but it still didn't stop. Pandemonium ensued as more officers appeared and tried to intervene, only to be beaten off by the runaway's flailing arms, one of them wielding a large oil can and another hitting out with a metal hose key. There was no way they could have got out via the main gate, but that was not their objective. The driver swung the wheel and the vehicle veered left past the hospital, demolishing a low wall and some railings as it did so, and picked up speed downhill in a circular path inside the boundary wall. They were making for the football pitch and a second, unmanned gate adjacent to it at the rear of the prison. This back exit led to the prison farm and comprised two sets of high double doors, one of solid wood, the other one of steel, both locked and bolted. The fugitives had made up their minds to take this way out and proceeded to do so in heroic fashion. Using the length of the pitch to gather more speed, the tanker was driven straight at the gates and there was the sound of splintered wood as the doors were torn off their hinges by the impact. Then there was a crashing of metal as the second pair of doors gave way,

"Jennings' Taxi" (Courtesy Simon Dell M.B.E.)

extensively damaging the tanker and injuring the escapees with splinters of flying glass from the windscreen and windows. They were outside now on a rough track leading to the Rundlestone-Two Bridges road and the driver raced for the road, reaching the gate leading to it just in time for a quick thinking Moore to run out and flag down a passing car. The driver innocently stopped to ask what was wrong, only to be dragged from his vehicle by the escapees who then piled in and drove off. Someone had called out "Don't use any violence!" and a relieved motorist found himself unharmed at the side of the road but nevertheless dismayed to see his car disappearing in the distance towards Two Bridges. Three prisoners, two of them of a violent disposition, had got clean away from the heart of Dartmoor prison in a matter of minutes and in broad daylight.

By now the alarm had been raised and soon there were police check points and search parties organised. Police with tracker dogs were sent from as far away as Honiton and Torquay to reinforce the Tavistock contingent and prison officers looking for the missing men. We do not know what Jennings and his companions intended once they were free, but having accomplished the most difficult and dangerous part of their plan, their luck ran out. The stolen car was found to be low on petrol, forcing them to do the only thing they could do — look for somewhere to hide. At Postbridge they turned right towards Widecombe-in-the-Moor and drove to Soussons Common, most of which was not a common at all, but comprised over 600 acres of fir plantations. The car was concealed with branches and ferns as the runaways, knowing the police road checks would be scaled down after twenty-four hours if they weren't found, prepared to lie low. Again luck was against them because they'd been seen entering the area by two forestry workers who, when they heard about the escape, returned and found the car under its camouflage covering. The police were alerted and by 1.00pm they were ready to tackle the enormous task confronting them — how to flush out three desperate men hiding in a vast wood. Fortunately help was at hand; a Territorial Army unit from Kent, based at Okehampton Camp, who were exercising on the moor, willingly abandoned their 'war' to help with the search.

It was the 'Terriers' who had the greatest success. The Soussons Wood conifers at that time were only 4 feet to 10 feet high with thick undergrowth and ferns which made the search a long and tedious affair. The area was divided into 'squares' and systematically combed by the combined forces. It took five hours to do it. Two young soldiers stumbled on Matthews who was lying concealed in the undergrowth, and despite a frantic effort to get away, during which he aimed a blow at one of them, they managed to hold him until prison officers rushed in and took him into custody. Shortly afterwards Jennings was located by police dog Astor, and was recaptured. Moore was the last to be caught, by another T.A. soldier. He had a weak heart and made no resistance as he was handed over to be taken back to Dartmoor.

Jennings, Matthews, and Moore all appeared at Devon Assizes later that year charged with:
1. Taking and driving away a tanker without the owner's consent.
2. Malicious damage to prison property.
3. Escaping from HM Prison. (every escapee faced the Magistrates on this charge at that time. Today jurisdiction is in the hands of the prison Governor).

They were each found 'Guilty as charged' and sentenced to six months, nine months, and fifteen months imprisonment, to run concurrently, but to be consecutive to, the sentences already being served.

It was an ignominious ending to an amazing break out. The trio have long since left the 'moor', but Jennings, who seemed to have been the ringleader, is still remembered when prison officers who served at Dartmoor get to yarning about the day three prisoners went for a ride in 'Jennings' Taxi'.

A TWIST IN THE TALE

Years ago the life of a country 'Bobby' was not the idyllic dream many people think it was. The job entailed long hours and trips to remote areas in every kind of weather, working alone and unsupervised, never knowing when he might be called out, perhaps from a warm bed in winter, to investigate an occurrence. When Princetown had a resident policeman he had the additional responsibility of liasing with Dartmoor prison, and was the first in line to receive information and descriptions of escaped prisoners. He then passed the information to Force Headquarters in Exeter who would inform all neighbouring Police Forces and co-ordinate a search.

Just after midnight on 26 September 1966, P.C.Roper was roused from slumber by a telephone call from the prison to say a car had been abandoned near the prison entrance, a suspicious circumstance in itself with obvious implications. He went at once to the prison and found the vehicle, a Vauxhall saloon, unlocked and with the ignition key missing. He then checked the licence number with Police H.Q. Information Room who told him the car was owned by someone living in the Torquay area. Constable Roper decided to call up the night duty Patrol Car, and arrange for a watch to be kept on the Vauxhall. Then, accompanied by a Prison Officer, he searched the area, including the prison quarry half a mile distant. There was no sign of the car driver or anyone else, but they did see a light on prison land in the direction of the Rundlestone - Two Bridges road. It was evident they could be dealing with an escape attempt with help from outside the jail. However, on their return to the prison, they met the Patrol Car crew who reported having stopped and questioned a man they'd seen at Merrivale, walking towards Tavistock. He turned out to be a cafe owner in the town, heading for home after abandoning a car at Princetown which, he claimed, had run out of petrol. Furthermore, he said he had borrowed the car from a friend in Torquay and correctly identified the owner of the Vauxhall. An examination revealed the petrol tank was indeed empty and the mystery appeared to be solved.

The Constable returned to his police station home in the village, only to receive another call from the prison at 4.45am informing him an escape attempt had in fact been made that night! Once again he went out into the morning blackness to get the details. The incident with the abandoned car, together with the mysterious light that was seen earlier, had alerted the prison staff to the possibility that 'something was going on', and so it proved to be. In the early hours of that morning, the prison Yard Patrol heard footsteps outside the boundary wall and at the same time noticed two cell windows with the bars missing. An investigation revealed the occupants, McManus and Russell, in possession of a 'rope' made out of twisted sheets and blankets, and obviously about to abscond. It was a classic 'story book' escapade. Tavistock police with dogs were called up to search the vicinity of the prison, and although nothing suspicious was found, they remained there until daybreak. Later on, the man who had been stopped and questioned the night before came to collect the Vauxhall, which was still under observation. After further questioning it was apparent that by an amazing coincidence, he had been forced to leave the car because he'd run out of petrol on the very night two convicted men in Dartmoor prison were actively engaged in breaking out!

An unlucky motorist who had to abandon his car caused a police investigation which, though fruitless in itself, had helped thwart a determined escape attempt.

THE HUNTERS AND THE HUNTED

The task of searching for escaped prisoners has always rested with the police force. Prison warders worked closely with the police, manning road blocks and assisting in searches as directed by them, but if the escapees were still at large two or three days later, they were recalled to run the prison and the local Constabulary assumed sole responsibility.

Prior to 1966 Dartmoor prison did not have radio communications, a dog section, or an internal security fence. In addition there was a more dangerous and desperate type of criminal interned there, many of them serving long sentences and therefore highly motivated towards escaping. Nearly every escapee who did abscond did so in the winter when the weather was at its worst or under cover of mist and the long nights. Those engaged in looking for them faced almost unbearable hardships, turning out at a moment's notice (the Tavistock police abandoned their annual Christmas Dinner on one occasion) to face long hours manning isolated checkpoints or tramping over the moors, perhaps in torrents of rain, sleet, or snow, with icy winds that cut through their uniforms (they were not issued with extra protective clothing). It was worse for the fugitives, who were even less adequately clad, and unsure of their whereabouts. Policemen long retired have a fund of horror stories about their experiences, some of which would be held in doubt had they been told by someone other than a trusted 'Bobby'.

On one occasion two escapees were found by police cowering in the snow, half-frozen, and actually crying with pain in the cold. Another prisoner, desperate for food, tore the leg off a dead sheep and ate the raw meat; yet another consumed some candles he found in an old farmhouse where he took shelter.

For the hunters there was no shelter. Policemen were posted to lonely cross-roads and bridges to maintain a vigil for as long as was necessary, perhaps several days, and were expected to remain there until relieved. These duties were often shared by prison warders, but there were times when the police had to go it alone. One old-timer, ex Sgt. Ken Northey of Tavistock, recalls spending fourteen hours at Moorshop on the edge of Dartmoor, in the dark, in a snowstorm, alone and without refreshment. By morning he was so cold he sought the meagre shelter of the nearest ditch and kept watch from there. He had to face the uncompromising wrath of his Inspector when he turned up next morning. Another policeman was manning a bridge overlooking the railway on the outskirts of Tavistock. After enduring a cold, lonely night, and with snow falling, he was delighted when in the morning a baker's van delivering freshly made pasties to Tavistock, stopped and the driver offered him one. When he looked inside he discovered his 'hot fresh pasties' were frozen and covered in a layer of snow that had penetrated the cracks in the doors. Nevertheless, with commendable determination, a ravenous constable managed to find a palatable pasty at the bottom of the pile, and claims a world record time for devouring it!

Hunting an escaped prisoner. P.C. Joe Gater handling bloodhound "Turpin" followed by P.C. Reg Borlase.

The popular notion of officers chasing fugitives over the moors in a mist with bloodhounds straining at the leash is only partly true. Neither the prison nor the police had bloodhounds to employ, but there were at least two generous sources from which help came from time to time. In the 1920s a Miss Lowe of Minions, near Liskeard, Cornwall, loaned three hounds to help police and warders hunt down two desperate escapees. They were directed and controlled by a Miss Clarke, and although they were not directly responsible for recapturing the two men, the dogs proved invaluable in guiding search parties all the way from Princetown to Roborough Down in driving wind and rain along the very route they'd taken, as was proved by the discovery of their discarded prison clothing. Both men were later apprehended in Plymouth. From 1946 until 1953 assistance was freely given by Mrs. H.M.Blakiston of Bratton Tor Kennels, Bratton Clovelly (and later of Lydford) who bred bloodhounds. This lady knew, as did Miss Lowe and Miss Clarke before her, that hounds only worked to advantage under the direction of their owners; consequently she accompanied the police on many occasions, sometimes across rough country, often at night and in bad weather. A former traffic policeman, Mr. R. Borlase, recalls sending a car to Bratton Clovelly to collect bloodhounds and the resident Constable (the late Mr.J.Gater) immediately the force was informed a prisoner was at large. P.C. Gater got to know the dogs well and became proficient in handling them himself, especially a hound named 'Turpin'. Mrs. Blakiston had paid 75 guineas for him and trained him herself

P.C. Gater and Turpin 1948/52, convict hunt. P.C. Borlase (flat cap), P.C. Easterbrook and another.

specially for tracking. It was P.C. Joe Gaiter who, with P.C. Brian Kendrick, was responsible for forming the Devon Constabulary dog unit in the late 1950s, based in Torquay. In 1964, the unit was extended to other stations, including Tavistock. They used Alsatians who could not only track, but were capable of apprehending an escapee until their handlers caught up with them. Dartmoor prison followed suit (on the recommendation of the Mountbatten Enquiry after Frank Mitchell's escape in 1966) and police dogs, with their handlers, manned the prison for several months to enable prison officers and dogs to be trained. The prison dog section still plays a prominent role in security.

For more than 60 years the Devon police have worked to guidelines set out in an 'Escape Scheme' devised by a remarkable man, Major Lyndon Henry Morris, CBE, MC, DL. He was the Governor of Dartmoor prison (the youngest ever to hold that position) prior to taking up the post of Chief Constable of Devon on 2 April 1931 He was therefore well qualified to organise a system that has been successful for so long and is still in use, with amendments, today. For security reasons the details cannot be revealed except to say the plan involved sealing off the moor, setting up roadside check points, and directing search parties from a Central Control Room. Police helicopters are an essential part of every escape operation today.

A convict hunt used to be the only occasion when policemen could claim overtime, after all available resources and the Special Constabulary had been mobilised. The 'Specials' are a voluntary force, but no less enthusiastic for that. The author remembers one Special Constable — his father-in-law, the late Mr. E. J. Batten of Brentor — spending many a cold winter night keeping watch on the railway lines at Brentor station, turning out after working all day as usual. On one occasion 'Rubber Bones Webb', a famous Dartmoor escapee, boarded a train at Brentor station and got clear of the county. By tradition the policeman who actually caught an escaped prisoner had the privilege of returning him to Dartmoor, and on at least one occasion it was a 'Special' who did the honours.

One might think that after all the inconveniences and privations endured in order to capture them, prisoners would receive little sympathy from their captors. In fact the opposite has often been the case. The pitiful condition some escapees have been found in have aroused the finest instincts in the policemen involved, who are on record as having had a 'whip-round' at the station to nip along to the nearest cafe or fish and chip shop to buy a hot meal for a starving prisoner. Others have been plied with sandwiches and endless mugs of tea whilst cheerful banter was often exchanged in the aftermath of a successful 'hunt'. I quote the words of an 'old lag' ('Rubber Bones', writing in 'The People' Sunday newspaper after his release from prison) who was recaptured near Okehampton wet through, starving, and exhausted, after three days on the run in freezing November weather: "After my capture kind arms took hold of me — the arms of the Devon Constabulary. 'Poor devil', said one. 'He must be nearly dead.' said another. Then I found a paper bag full of cakes in one hand and an orange in the other, whilst a cigarette was being thrust in my mouth and someone else was lighting it. I'll never forget those grand, fine policemen." After describing being taken to Tavistock police station, he concluded: "I did not stay long in that dream world. Very soon two warders arrived from Dartmoor prison." All of which sums up very well the usual conclusion to a Dartmoor escape.

RED FACES

Convicts are escorted from the prison for work on the farm or quarry.

Prison work parties are still seen in Princetown and on the prison farm, but not in such large numbers or as often as in the past. One day, in the 1960s, a party was at work painting what is now the High Moorland Visitor's Centre, known then simply as 'The Duchy' when the old Duchy Hotel was the Prison Officer's Mess and had accommodation for bachelor warders. When the supervising officer's back was turned, one of the inmates who was working from a ladder, descended, and after a quick look around, ran up Plymouth Road towards the moor as fast as his legs would go. He thought the 'coast was clear' but it wasn't. He was seen by a Princetown resident who ran all the way to the prison main entrance to raise the alarm, only to be told: "Escaped prisoner from outside the 'Duchy', full of prison officers — don't be bloody daft!" and the door slammed shut.

Not long afterwards there was a 'hue and cry' when the word was passed "There's one away!" There were red faces in the 'nick' that day, and they stayed resolutely inside.

Convicts parade for work at Dartmoor Prison, 1911.
Courtesy B. Jones.

THE FRENCH AT DARTMOOR

Every prison has a high wall around it and Dartmoor had two such walls when it opened as a French Prisoner of War Depot in 1809. The inner wall had platforms for the soldier guards who kept watch over the interior and who didn't hesitate to shoot or bayonet anyone trying to escape. Most of the prisoners in those early days were sailors, among them crews of privateers, vicious desperadoes who would stop at nothing in an effort to escape. Under cover of darkness, mist or heavy rain, many a man, sometimes groups of men, found a way of scaling the boundary walls undetected. This was an achievement in itself, because there were wires strung around the walls with bells suspended from them. If the wire was disturbed, the jangling of the bells was the signal for Drummers to beat 'To Arms!' Then every guard, on or off duty, armed himself and rushed to apprehend the escapees. In 1810 the Nottinghamshire Militia arrived at Dartmoor and several French prisoners, seeking to take advantage of the new arrival's supposed lack of vigilance on their first night on guard duty, attempted a mass escape, but were detected milling about in the area between the two walls known as the 'Military Walk'. When the alarm was given, every Militiaman, some half-clothed, ran to the scene and the escape bid was foiled.

The previous year in a similar incident involving the Lancashire Militia an officer's servant who had turned out without his full uniform was mistaken for a prisoner and bayoneted to death. These occurrences emphasise the ruthlessness with which escaping prisoners were dealt.

A Dartmoor prisoner of war attempting to escape had a lot more than the stone walls, alarm bells, and armed sentries to contend with. There was the moor to cross, without signposts, and a population ranged against him, either for fear of punishment if they helped him, or the possibility of a £5 reward if they turned him in. The tors and bogs made travel difficult and there was little shelter; besides a man needed rest, food, and the means of crossing the Channel. Torbay was usually their objective, where there was a chance of stealing a boat, or maybe persuading a fisherman to take them to France (fishermen on both sides were, by mutual agreement, immune from hostilities during the French wars). Occasionally boats and their occupants were 'hijacked' and forced to sail to France under threat of death. Eventually things got so bad the Admiralty ordered all unattended vessels on the south coast to have their oars and sails removed as a precaution against theft by escaping POWs.

Smugglers were involved in the escape trade, and 'trade' is precisely what developed when professional 'escape agents' began to appear. These men were unscrupulous scallywags who would arrange everything for an escapee for a price. Lucky customers were whisked away to somewhere safe, perhaps an isolated house or a quiet inn with an understanding (and equally expensive) landlord who would arrange transportation to France. Sometimes things could go tragically wrong though. On 26 January 1811 five French officers living on Parole in Moretonhampstead stole away from their lodgings after dark and met a local Carrier called Richard Tapper who had horses waiting to take them to Topsham on the River Exe near Exeter. There they were joined by two well known smugglers from Cheriton Bishop, brothers Thomas and William Vinnicombe, who for a down payment of £25 and the promise of another £250, took them on board their boat and set sail down the river for France. At the mouth of the river their luck ran out when the vessel ran aground off Exmouth and they were caught. The French officers, three of whom were ship's captains, were sent to Plymouth, probably to Mill Prison. Tapper and the Vinnicombes were tried at the Devon Assizes in the summer of 1812 and sentenced to transportation for life.

At Dartmoor a number of prisoners were employed outside the prison on road making and various building projects that included the Church and Parsonage. They were paid sixpence a day, but, as reported by the Americans who took over when the French war ended, payment was made every three months and not at all if there was an escape during that period. That didn't stop determined men. One bold Frenchman effected a unique method of escape when his colleagues encased him in a recess in the chimney they were constructing in the Parsonage and walled him in, leaving air holes in loose mortar, and successfully concealing his absence at roll call. The prisoner waited until they departed at the end of the day, forced his way out (the mortar not having had time to set) and made his getaway. The question might be asked: what motivated his companions, knowing they faced certain punishment when he was found to be missing?

As already mentioned, heavy penalties were inflicted on sentries who aided escapees. In addition, a barrier of iron railings inside the inner wall prevented prisoners from approaching the guards and fraternising with them, and maybe bribing them for help in escaping. It did no good because several instances of bribery came to light as well as an unknown number that didn't. In 1812 three French prisoners paid a Roscommons Militiaman £2, the going rate at the time, to help them 'over the wall'. Paddy wasn't the only one among the rank and file who had no scruples about supplementing his pay in this manner. Soldiers were poorly paid and conscripted from the lowest classes, drunkards almost to a man, so it was no surprise to find so many of them willing to risk a flogging, or

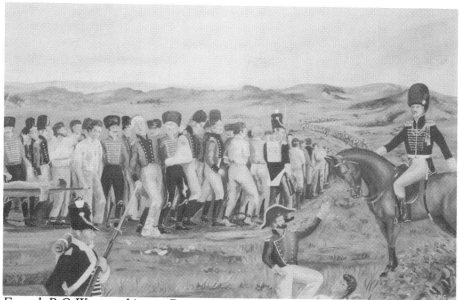

French P.O.Ws marching to Dartmoor Depot under escort.
From a painting by an unknown prisoner at Dartmoor Prison.

perhaps their lives, for the price of a drink. There was a sting in the tail though; the Irishman was detected trying to pass forged notes, the price of his treachery, at the daily market that was held within the prison. Forgery was a big problem in every prisoner of war depot and the death penalty had been introduced to try and stop it. The forger, a prisoner called Lustique, was later identified and both he and the soldier were tried and hanged.

On a lighter note, the best known story is that of 'Le Capitaine Calonne et sa Dame' — the title of a play performed by the prisoners. Theatricals were a prominent feature of prison life and performances were often attended by the British. On this occasion a certain officer and his wife generously offered to help by lending the leading actors a uniform and female clothing. The offer was gladly accepted and the performance was a huge success until, towards the end, an announcement was made: "Messieurs, the Captain and his wife have left the prison." The implication was clear and only too true — the French 'Captain and his wife' had passed unchallenged out of the main prison entrance to freedom, leaving an embarrassed officer and his lady having to endure hoots and whistles of derision from a delighted prisoner audience!

THE INSPECTOR

A prisoner escaped from a work party outside Dartmoor prison several years ago and later stole a car. Meanwhile, police check points were set up and every road leading off the moor was quickly sealed. The check point at Moorshop, between Tavistock and Princetown was particularly busy and there was a long 'tailback' of vehicles waiting to be checked when a Plymouth Police Inspector arrived on the scene. He found his men coping well, but having to deal with a number of impatient motorists and, as sometimes happens, one or two tried to sneak past, pretending they were unaware they had to stop the same as everybody else. One car crawled by on the outside without stopping and incurred the extreme displeasure of the inspector who ticked him off before sending him on his way with a proverbial 'flea in his ear'.

Later on, back at the station, a tired and irate Inspector tossed his cap onto his desk muttering about the impatient oaf in the blue Morris 1000 who didn't have the sense to realise everyone had to be checked and deliberately 'jumped' the queue. There was a ghastly silence. "Did you say a blue Morris 1000 Sir?" a voice said, "the man we're looking for stole one at Princetown." There was a flurry of activity as the details and direction the car was heading in were circulated. The vehicle was soon found, not far from where it was last seen, but there was no sign of the wanted man who had somehow eluded the police cordon and disappeared (he was eventually detected somewhere in France and returned to custody, having earned a prominent place in Dartmoor's escape records).

Now that a respectable period of time has elapsed, the story can be told, but in Devon today there is a Senior Police Officer who would prefer to forget this particular incident.

FACING THE ODDS

A runaway prisoner forced to keep on the move by search parties faces formidable odds on Dartmoor. The beautiful moors seen by tourists conceal a variety of dangers: lurking in the hillsides are old turf-ties, up to eight feet deep in places; rock clitters where you risk breaking an ankle or a leg at every step; old mine workings and quarries; and of course the bogs which feed the Dartmoor streams. They are all traps for the unwary. Then there are the tors, intersected by leats and rivers. Imagine fleeing across such a landscape in a rainstorm, poorly clad, perhaps at night with a biting cold wind and nowhere to shelter. Dozens of escapees have ended up in barns, haystacks, even pig pens, at the end of their tether, hungry and wet through, to be discovered by farmers who more often than not have warmed them and fed them before handing them over to the authorities. Others have not been so lucky.

The winter of 1853 on Dartmoor was awesome in its severity. Princetown and the prison were isolated by deep snow, the water supply was frozen, and 1000 prisoners were on a reduced diet because the supply wagons were unable to get through. On 14 February the situation was desperate and gangs of convicts were sent to try and clear the roads. The cold was so intense the soldier guards were permitted to stand 'sideways to the wind' when, incredibly, a convict took advantage of their restricted vision to abscond, and although he was spotted and hotly pursued, he escaped into the white wilderness of the moor. The conditions were so awful the guards went unpunished, a rare concession on the part of their officers.

Only the convict's name has come down to us in the records. John Brown survived and got as far as Peter Tavy, having crossed seven miles of snowbound moorland before collapsing in a farmyard. The farmer who found him handed him over to the police and got the £5 reward payable. The next day, Captain Gambier, the prison's first convict prison Governor, received a message from Dr. Pearce of Tavistock Infirmary to say Brown's return to prison would be delayed — he was badly frost-bitten and had several toes amputated. Whether through foolishness or bravery, this convict paid a terrible price for an opportunist escape.

An unconfirmed report of that period tells of an escaped convict observed by warders picking his way across Fox Tor mires, one of the most dangerous bogs on Dartmoor. They declined to follow as a lowering mist quickly hid him from view. He was never seen again and was presumed drowned in 'Dartmoor Stables' as the mires were called then on account of the number of ponies and cattle swallowed up by them each year. Several fugitives have vanished on the moor in the past and we can be sure some of them perished either in the bogs or in the rivers in flood. A delightful moor land stream can turn into a terrifying torrent after a winter storm, sweeping everything before it including trees and boulders.

In all the recorded escapes from Dartmoor in modern times no woman has been violated or any attempt made to harm a resident. Some wayfarers have been robbed it's true, and on one occasion a motorist was bundled out of his car (see 'Jennings Taxi'), but even then one of the escapees called out "No violence!" All the same, for an elderly man to be woken at 3.00am by a six foot tall escaped prisoner must have been an unnerving experience, although 75 year old Mr. Ernest Worth afterwards declared he and his wife Elsie never had cause to be scared of him. It happened on Friday 19 August 1960 and the convict, George Norman, 30, was "Nigh on done up." as Mr. Worth put it, after running away from a farm party twelve hours previously. For all his exertions, Norman was at Peat Cot, just outside Princetown and only a couple of miles or so from the prison. This was a prime example of an 'opportunist' escape, and for domestic reasons: his wife was threatening to leave him he told Mr. Worth, and he was

Convicts taking shelter on the moor, 1870s.
Courtesy Dartmoor Prison Museum.

concerned about his child. Norman was serving a six year sentence for housebreaking, but he didn't break into the Worth's home — he didn't have to because they never locked the door. An unbelievable situation then developed. Whilst the police and prison officers with tracker dogs were tramping over the moors looking for him, Norman made himself at home and opened his heart to Mr. Worth, who thought his surprise visitor "Had a good spark in him." His 'visitor' stayed for two hours, during which time Mrs. Worth made tea and her husband "Talked to him like a father." Rested and refreshed, the prisoner thanked them and shook hands. "I told him to return and finish his sentence." Mr. Worth said, but he didn't — instead he made off over the moor, enabling the old chap to go to his brother's house a short distance away and telephone the police. The search parties then congregated in the Peat Cot area, but to no avail; their man had a good start, and unknown to them, was heading south.

Twelve hours later, having crossed some of the most desolate parts of Dartmoor, he was challenged by a farmer, Mr. C. Woodley of Yadsworthy Farm near Cornwood, who saw him on his land. He came quietly, he'd had enough. Like so many before him he had lost a tussle with 'old Dartymoor'.

There was one convict though, an elderly man, who knew precisely where to go after bolting from a work party one foggy day over 100 years ago. He came from Islington, near Bovey Tracey, and thought it would be the last place his pursuers would look for him. He was lucky enough to come across a scarecrow in a moorland newtake* and, burying his convict clothes, donned the old clothes it had on. Then he saw a hoe lying nearby and promptly took it before setting off along the road to Islington for all the world like a labourer going to his work. However, on arrival at his home, imagining no doubt a warm welcome and a good dinner, his wife refused to let him in and drove him away, threatening to summon the Constable (one version of this story says she actually did so and claimed the £5 reward for his subsequent arrest!).

A disillusioned husband skulked about the neighbourhood for a day or two and was recaptured, having succumbed to odds of a very different kind, but at the same time establishing another legend in the escape annals of the 'moor'.
* Newtake = A walled enclosure or field.

CAUGHT IN TAVISTOCK

What must have been one of the shortest convict hunts on record occurred on 23 April 1959 when William Bright escaped from Dartmoor. At 6.00 am that day, before his escape was known about, he was seen loitering in the vicinity of Tavistock South railway station (since closed), and the police were informed. Their informant was a very well known Tavistock man, Mr. Tommy Smale of Sunshine Terrace, who was unaware of the man's identity of course, but thought it suspicious for a stranger to be there so early in the day. The incident was duly noted, and when the police were told about Bright's escape later that morning, they were able to contain him and subsequently recapture him.

Their gratitude for the 'tip-off' was expressed in a personal letter to Mr. Smale from Plympton Police Superintendent A. Roper. Tommy carried the letter in his wallet for more than 20 years, when he proudly showed it to Tavistock Police Inspector D. Roper (Superintendent Roper's nephew), who in turn showed it to the author — which is how this little tale came to be written.

DEVON CONSTABULARY

TELEPHONE No. 3110.

Our Ref. CID/PGD.

Your Ref.

Criminal Investigation Dept.,

"E" Division,

PLYMPTON.

2nd. June, 1959.

Dear Sir,

     Re: William BRIGHT.

    With reference to the escape from Dartmoor Prison, Princetown, of the above named convict on the 23rd. April, 1959, it has been brought to my notice of the assistance which you rendered to the Police in this matter.

    At 6am. on the 23rd. April, 1959, when you saw BRIGHT loitering at Tavistock South Railway Station there had been no indication that a convict had escaped from the Prison. However, by your action in reporting this incident to the Police, we had some knowledge of BRIGHT's whereabouts when his escape was later discovered.

    This made it possible to contain him in the area and subsequently led to his recapture.

    I am therefore taking this opportunity to express my appreciation of the assistance which you rendered in this matter.

                Yours faithfully,

                Superintendent.

Mr. T. SMALE,
No. 11 Sunshine Terrace,
Parkwood Road,
TAVISTOCK.

A VERY UNSAVOURY EPISODE

Prisoners who are determined to escape have an abundance of time in which to contemplate how it might be done, and when a strategy has been decided on it only requires the right circumstances to occur for it to be put into effect. Vigilance is something the prison staff are trained for and strive for, but as in any occupation, it sometimes happens there is a distraction or pressure of work which can cause a lapse in security. An inmate with escape in mind is always on the lookout for just such an opportunity, and will take it.

Consider the prison kitchens. They are run by prison officer cooks, assisted by selected inmates, low category men who are considered trustworthy enough to work in an environment where kitchen knives, for example, are readily to hand. The meals are regular, a lot of the work is routine, and over a period of several months officers and inmates work together in harmony. A couple of times each week a contractor comes to remove the kitchen waste. At one time a local farmer took it away in steel drums for pig swill. "Here comes the man for his swill." the officer would say, and perhaps four inmates would be detailed to go outside and load the lorry. The driver was accompanied by a prison officer escort who supervised the job of getting the drums loaded as well as seeing the waste containers from the 'wings' were also emptied. He was responsible too for ensuring the inmates were returned to the kitchen, checking the load, and escorting the farmer off site. The officer cook would see his men back in and lock the security gates. If things were a bit hectic (as they are in every kitchen sometimes), he might feel he knew them well enough, when the lorry had gone, to ask "Is everyone back in?" Someone would say "Yes, Guv, we're all here." and the gates would be locked.

Now imagine a day when everything seems to be going wrong: they are behind schedule in the kitchen, it's sleeting outside in true Dartmoor fashion, and the farmer has come for his swill. After loading the lorry the inmates scuttle back inside, and a busy officer cook asks "Is everyone back in?" "We're all here, Guv." says a voice. But they're not — one of them is on the lorry inside a steel drum, having been concealed by his mates with discarded boxes, wrappings, and a sprinkling of kitchen waste. He relies on the escorting officer making just a cursory inspection of the drums in the atrocious weather, and it pays off, because he's clear of Princetown and on his way to Plymouth before he is missed. On the edge of the city the lorry pulls up at the first set of traffic lights, which are showing red, and our man pops out from his hiding place and makes off. He's unprepared for a prolonged spell of freedom though, and doesn't get far before he is captured by the police and returned to the prison. Nevertheless he has joined that select band of men who have successfully exploited a temporary chink in Dartmoor prison's security armour, and for a little while he will be something of a hero to his fellow prisoners.

This incident actually happened some years ago, except that the details about the officers involved and their part in it has been altered for the purpose of this story, which is to illustrate the sort of thing that can happen if an officer allows himself to be distracted or fails to pay full attention to his duties. The disposal of waste is carried out differently these days, and work practices are constantly under review, especially after an event like the one you have just read about. As for the escapee, he surely deserves ten out of ten for determination and fortitude by enduring the stink of a well used swill bin. It must have lingered about his person long enough (and strong enough) to draw attention to him, thereby making the task of recognising and apprehending him a lot easier!

AN UNHAPPY CHRISTMAS.

Christmas is the worst time of year in any prison. Inmate's thoughts naturally are with their loved ones, and many a man has cracked under the strain and made a run for it, often with little chance of success.

In the nineteenth century ago every fit and able man at Dartmoor began his sentence working in the prison quarry, or on reclamation work on the boglands, preparing the ground for cultivation. Christmas Eve 1896 was no exception and a work party set out as usual for a day digging near the Blackabrook river, among them three men who had made up their minds to run for it at the first opportunity. One of them was William Carter, beginning a twelve year sentence for robbery with violence and who had a wife he hadn't seen for months. His fellow conspirators were Ralph Goodwin, serving five years for burglary, and another burglar, John Martin, who had twelve years ahead of him. All three were desperate and determined men willing to risk being shot in order to get away from the living hell that was Dartmoor prison.

It was a murky day on the moor and by 11.00a.m. a mist had closed in, almost obscuring the prison buildings, and with visibility fast deteriorating the guards decided to return to the prison. As the men marched back, the trio bent on escaping could see this was their only chance, and on a signal from Carter, they threw handfuls of earth into the faces of their escort before running for the cover of a fir plantation they were approaching. The Civil Guard, who were mostly ex-army men, opened fire and Carter fell dead, shot in the back. He was just 22 years old. Martin and Goodwin made it to the woods with the guards in pursuit. Martin was cornered, mouthing defiance and threatening them with a stone he was holding, when a quick acting warder closed in and knocked him down with his truncheon. In exchange for a few brief minutes of freedom he had forfeited his remission and faced the punishment cells on his return to prison.

Goodwin vanished into the gloom and spent the rest of that day and the night scurrying over the moor trying to get as far away as possible before daylight came again. Splashing through rivers, and sometimes sinking up to his waist in the bogs, he managed to keep going until dawn, when he saw the blurred outline of some buildings and assumed he must be near to Plymouth. No such luck, with despair in his heart he recognised the grim shape of Dartmoor prison! He had wandered in a circle in the mist, and was walking the streets of Princetown.

But for the fear of getting shot in the process, he'd have given himself up; instead he decided to run for it once more. It was a cold, clear Christmas Day, and the warders who were watching for him spotted him clambering over a distant tor. He in turn saw the sun glinting on their field glasses and waved his hat to them in defiance. His priority now was to get a change of clothing, and this he did by breaking into two houses at Postbridge that night. His haul included a change of clothing and a pair of boots, which enabled him to dispose of the prison issue ones with the broad arrow hammered into the soles. Then despite being tired and hungry, he doubled back on his tracks to Tavistock. There, on Boxing Day, he raided another house and was lucky enough to discover the remains of a Christmas dinner, including some cold turkey, plum pudding, and other good things. Then, after good feed, he found the railway line and followed it to Plymouth.

By morning he was at Devonport, and at Camels Head he decided to leave the railway and take to the streets only to find he was unavoidably walking towards a policeman with a dog. The Constable wished him a cheery "Good morning." and Goodman replied without arousing any curiosity, but when the dog ran playfully after him he mistakenly thought the game was up and ran off, with a now suspicious 'Bobby' in pursuit. It was a short chase because the fugitive was just about 'all in'. In desperation he turned, flourishing a knife he'd stolen at Postbridge, and threatened dire consequences if the policeman came any closer. Pretending he had a gun, a quick thinking officer said he would shoot him down, upon which Goodman surrendered.

After being returned to Dartmoor prison he was called upon to give evidence at the inquest on young Carter who was shot and killed. He was still in a state of exhaustion with badly blistered feet, so was allowed to sit throughout the proceedings. The jury's verdict was predictable: 'Justifiable Homicide'. Ralph Goodwin had exhibited exceptional stamina and suffered much hardship in his escape bid, only to be caught after momentarily losing his nerve and with success within his grasp. William Carter would have been buried in an unmarked grave in Princetown churchyard in the plot set aside for dead convicts. Christmas in prison can never be 'Happy', and it was even less so at Dartmoor that year.

MAKING A RUN FOR IT

"It always happens when you least expect it." commented Senior Officer (Works) Jon Dunne, recalling an escape incident in which he played a leading part. On 8 June 1988 two inmates, David Meads, 44, and 26-year-old Terence Poole, escaped from the prison Blacksmith shop. In the rear wall of the workshop was a barred window overlooking the walkway between the boundary wall and the inner security fence. The window was a 'weak spot' which the two men identified and planned to exploit.

Security in the shop was difficult to monitor because it contained several protective screens which were used to shield other inmates working there when welding was being done. Poole and Meads had manufactured a metal ladder and concealed it among numerous other items in the shop. On the morning of their escape they contrived to work behind a screen adjacent to the window, and at a moment when their supervisors were busy with other inmates they used oxyacetylene torches to quickly cut through the bars. Taking the ladder they had made, they got out through the window and ran to the 18 ft high wall. They had misjudged the height though, and found the ladder was too short, so after climbing onto the top of the wall they were forced to jump down the other side. It was the undoing of the older man because in landing, Meads injured his ankle.

They were spotted almost immediately as they fled past the prison farm. Mr. Dunne was working nearby when a civilian worker who was running to raise the alarm gasped: "There's two away!" Then he saw the escapees running for the woods, which at that time covered an extensive area between the prison and Rundlestone (nearly every tree was blown down in the winter gales of 1989). A prison officer dog handler was in pursuit, but between him and the fugitives was a damaged wire fence leaning towards him in such a way the dog was unable to get over it. Jon Dunne got over it though. He is a lifelong athlete and marathon runner and had dropped what he was doing to run and help. He soon overtook and detained Meads, who was hobbling. Poole vanished into the woods.

Another officer took Meads into custody, enabling Mr. Dunne to sprint through the trees after Poole, but the only person he saw was a colleague coming from the direction of Rundlestone. Neither of them had seen Poole but they were confident he hadn't crossed the road to the woods opposite. That information was invaluable to Acting Police Inspector B. Sobey when he arrived to supervise a search. With the police helicopter hovering overhead, the fugitive had no chance of making a run for it, and a thorough 'sweep' of the wood was organised. It was a difficult task with every tree in full leaf, and it was unsuccessful.

Accordingly, the combined force of police and prison officers carried out another search, which again was without result. At this point the Inspector asked Mr. Dunne if he was quite certain they had contained Poole, or was it just possible he'd got clear? "He's in there somewhere," he answered, "I'm sure of it." It was then decided to thoroughly cover the ground yet again, this time with additional men enlisted from the civilian staff at the prison, the first time they were ever involved in something like this.

When all was ready the mixed force, with dog handlers, moved off. Imagine their surprise when one of the dogs became agitated at the base of the very first tree they came to and heard his handler say: "What the 'ell are you doing up there — bird nesting?" A crestfallen Poole dropped to the ground from the branches where he'd been hiding, and the hunt was over before it had properly begun. He afterwards told officers he had recognised his pursuer, and knowing he couldn't outrun him, was forced to seek refuge up the tree where he was found. In fact pursuit was so swift he actually ducked behind a tree trunk as Mr. Dunne sped by and then climbed into the thick foliage where he had remained undetected for several hours, hoping he would get clean away. But for Inspector Sobey's persistence and faith in Jon Dunne's credibility he might have.

Poole and Meads had executed a cunning escape but hadn't bargained on being chased by an officer whose hobby is marathon running! By the way, after this inmates were unable to look out from the Blacksmith shop window — it was bricked up.

A BIZARRE DISGUISE

Imagine an undersized Fireman walking through a busy shopping centre wearing an extra large overcoat and a peaked cap several sizes too big for him. Would you view this apparition with suspicion? Of course you would, and what is more, if you saw a black face beneath the cap and the upturned collar at a time when coloured people were a rare sight in the Westcountry, you would be justified in feeling some amazement. Add to this the knowledge that a coloured inmate was on the run from Dartmoor prison and the thought that this could be him would rapidly come to mind. If you happened to be a policeman, suspicion, recognition, and reaction would be simultaneous — and they were, for the incident just described actually occurred. The fugitive, a 5 ft. tall West Indian, had somehow managed to evade the police cordon around the moor, and broke into Plympton Fire Station, taking an overcoat to cover his prison clothes, and a cap to complete what he hoped would be a disguise.

It was too obviously an impersonation and an over optimistic escapee was soon back behind bars at Dartmoor awaiting punishment for absconding.

JOE DENNY — THE MAN WHO BROKE *INTO* DARTMOOR PRISON

The story of how a coloured man, who was released from Dartmoor after serving an eight year sentence, returned the following year with the specific intention of breaking *into* the prison is without precedent and tinged with sadness. His motive was revenge for the alleged ill-treatment he had endured. During his subsequent trial the prosecution produced 124 prison reports against him for breaches of discipline, for which he was punished by flogging, solitary confinement, and periods on restricted diet (three days bread and water only). Was he persecuted because of his colour, as he claimed, or was he the troublesome nuisance the prison officials made him out to be? Many an officer today will tell you there are men in their charge who are sick in mind and should not be in prison at all. Whatever the truth may be, when a hardened criminal weeps in the dock, possibly with frustration at not being able to convince the court what he says is true, the reader may conclude there was cause to question a regime that broke men's hearts and led to several warders resigning year by year.

Prison conditions were harsh in the 19th century and the regulations laid down by the State applied to every prison, but Dartmoor's unique location high on a windswept moor, isolated it from the outside world. Consequently the regime was at the whim of those in charge. Outside work ceased only when there was heavy rain or snow, or because a Dartmoor mist restricted visibility and thus the degree of security. In addition, some discontented warders deliberately gave the convicts a hard time. It is against this background we should judge an episode which can only be described as bizarre. Joseph Denny had served time in three prisons:

Six months at Carmarthen Prison for housebreaking.

Seven years in Liverpool Jail for manslaughter.

Eight years at Dartmoor for felony.

After his release from Dartmoor prison on 8 January 1889 he spent nine months at sea, voyaging to the West Indies among other places. When he got back to England he set out on foot from London and made his way to Princetown seeking revenge for the alleged injustices he'd suffered at Dartmoor. In the summer of 1890 he was seen in the streets of Tavistock with a group of performing dogs and monkeys; he also turned up at Princetown where he presented his animal show on some waste ground the day before his escapade.

Just before midnight on Saturday 16 August the prison Governor, Capt. Oswald William Every, was making his final visit of the day to ensure all was well. Suddenly the alarm bells rang. The bells were activated by wires strung along the inside of the perimeter wall and were designed to detect anyone trying to escape. A search party was organised and Joe Denny was discovered hiding in the toilets adjacent to he carpenter's shop. He was recognised immediately by a surprised warder who exclaimed "Hello Joe! It's you isn't it?" When Denny could offer no explanation for being there he was handcuffed and handed over to the local policeman who lived in Princetown and had a 'lock up' in his house.

The prison Chaplain called next day (Sunday) but the constable was unwilling at first to open the cell door because of Denny's threatening manner. Denny had told him he had come to set fire to the prison and murder 'Flash Hardy', the Chief Warder, "And murder him I will!" he declared. The Chaplain, Rev. Clifford RickardsB.A., an experienced and kindly man, managed to calm the prisoner and give him some sound advice. He describes the interview and subsequent events in his book ('A Prison Chaplain on Dartmoor', E.Arnold, London, 1920) in a way that suggests he had a genuine sympathy for the fellow. Perhaps he knew about the alleged cruelty meted out to him in prison, over which of course he had no control.

Earlier that morning a prison farm worker found a dead sheep hidden in a cow shed; it had been bludgeoned to death and a large piece, cut from a shoulder, appeared to have been eaten raw. Denny admitted to this, saying: "I have done 15 years for the old woman and she ought to be able to stand a sheep or two." (Presumably the term 'old woman' referred to Queen Victoria). He was taken to Tavistock on Sunday afternoon and charged with prison breaking before Mr.W.S.Rosevere, who remanded him in custody until Tuesday 19 August. (It is interesting to note Denny was taken back to Princetown to be locked up because the River Tavy had recently burst its banks and the police cells, which were below river level, had been flooded). When he appeared before Mr. Rosevere again the charges were:

1. Breaking into Dartmoor prison for an unlawful purpose.
2. Being on prison premises for the purpose of setting fire to the building.
3. Killing and stealing a sheep, property of the prison authorities.

The newspapers described Denny as being a native of Barbados, about 44 years old, 'with a higher forehead than is usual for a Negro and intelligent features'. He was above average intelligence and wore spectacles which, in repose, gave him 'a benign look'. The courtroom was packed with spectators.

Evidence was given by the Governor, Capt. Oswald Every, Warder John Stacey, who had apprehended Denny, and Chief Warder Augustus Hardy, who produced a length of rope which, he said, must have been used by the defendant for the break in. It was a length of clothes line, one end of which had been attached to a post in the Deputy Governor's garden (his residence was adjacent to the boundary wall and to the left of the main prison entrance); the other end was hanging over the wall on the inside, presumably to enable the intruder to get back out. During the hearing the defendant was allowed to question witnesses, but had little to ask that was significant except when Mr. Hardy showed the court the rope.

Prisoner: "What was the length of rope hanging over the wall?"

Hardy: "I should think about six feet."

Prisoner: "A good drop for you!" (referring to a hanging).

There was uproar and laughing from onlookers and order was restored only by Mr. Rosevere threatening to clear the court. Denny was unable to contain his obvious resentment, shedding his 'benign appearance', and rendered a sweeping condemnation of Dartmoor prison. He described being put in irons and being confined to a dark cell because he was "A coloured man and plain spoken." The Chief Warder, he said, had put him through the most cruel punishments, being 'deputy governor, clergyman, doctor, and everything else'. In all the prisons he'd been in there was no officer given so much power as the Chief Warder at Dartmoor who had treated him worse than a dog. Despite warnings by the Magistrate "Not to be foolish," and "not to say any more," the defendant declared he could not get that man out of his mind. If he were released now, he went on "I could not leave until I put him in his grave." His idea had been to set fire to the prison, giving prisoners "A chance to escape from hell," and lie in wait for the Chief Warder, who would be the first to be called in case of fire, when he would have used the knife on him (he was relieved of a box of matches and a knife when he was arrested).

Throughout this tirade the prisoner glared at Mr. Hardy and repeated he "Would mount the gallows with a contented heart tomorrow." if he could send that rogue (pointing to the Chief Warder) before him. Denny was committed to the forthcoming Devon Assizes under the Larceny Act, having condemned himself. He was held at Exeter Prison until 2 December when he was brought before Judge Sir William Grantham. In the interim period the following letter was published in the 'Exeter Flying Post' dated 30 August:

'I wish to write a few lines about ex-convict Denny who is now awaiting trial for breaking into Dartmoor Prison. What he says in his statement is perfectly true. I was at Dartmoor with him for more than two years, and during the greater part of that tine he was under punishment. But for his iron constitution he would never have come out alive. He was several times flogged, and continually under bread and water. He was for several months wearing the black dress [1] and fourteen

---

1   'Black dress' — yellow and black uniform worn by convicts who either assaulted a warder or attempted to escape. The fourteen pounds of leg irons or chains were a practical deterrent.

pounds of iron chains, and in the winter of 1888 he was sent out to work on the bogs with a cold canvas dress [2] on... he was treated worse than a dog.'

The contents of this letter did not reach Denny and no mention of it was made at his trial. The prosecutor at the Assizes, after saying it was one of the most extraordinary cases he had ever encountered, proceeded to call witnesses who repeated the evidence they had given to the Tavistock magistrate. Chief Warder Hardy was interrupted several times by the defendant who complained about how cruelly he'd been treated by him. Mr. Hardy replied he had nothing to do with punishments or the withholding of privileges; his duty was to see reports were logged and he did not attend adjudications. When the defendant recalled being handcuffed and left in the cold whilst with a work party on the moor, Mr. Hardy said "If men refused to work they were handcuffed but were free to walk about". Capt. Every, the prison Governor, confirmed he had known the prisoner for a number of years, having had him in his custody, but denied saying "I expected as much." when Denny was apprehended, "We don't expect to find people trying to get inside," he remarked, "they generally try to get out!" (laughter in court). The Exeter Prison doctor testified how he had answered a complaint by Denny about being ill; in fact he had refused to eat and had to be removed to a special cell with a warder in attendance to ensure he ate and would be fit to appear in court. When the night watchman at Exeter said Denny had confessed to breaking into Dartmoor to get his revenge on the Chief Warder, Denny, in a desperate attempt to refute him said he'd often been told he talked in his sleep.

It was all downhill for the prisoner now, and when he addressed the jury he broke down and wept, acknowledging he had malice towards Mr. Hardy and had sought revenge, but he was then "In a passion." and asked for mercy, being a coloured man far from his native land. Judge Grantham was unmoved. Dartmoor prison's Governor had acted with great discretion, kindness, and consideration for him, he said. Chief Warder Hardy could not give effect to any ill feeling he might have had, declared the Judge, and he did not see he had any ill feeling. He sentenced Denny to 12 months hard labour (at least he didn't award him penal servitude, which would have meant his returning to Dartmoor).

Joe Denny died in prison. For all his misdeeds, he may have been harbouring a genuine grievance, and died a broken man; maybe the physical effects of the punishments he'd received accelerated his demise; perhaps he was mentally unbalanced. Whatever the truth of the matter, his story is a frightening indictment of the penal system in Victorian England, and goes a long way towards explaining why a man broke *into* Dartmoor prison after getting *out*.

---

2   'Canvas dress' — worn by convicts who, as a means of protest tore up their clothes.

SOURCES:

Western Morning News, Evening Herald

Trewmans Exeter Flying Post

Tavistock Times, Tavistock Gazette

Sunday Mirror

Daily Mail

News Chronicle

Notes and Queries (various).

Prisoners of War in Britain 1756-1815 (Francis Abell).Milford.
     Oxford University Press.

The Story of Dartmoor Prison (Basil Thomson).W. Heinemann 1910.

A Prison Chaplain on Dartmoor (Rev. Rickards, M.D.). Edward Arnold, London 1920.

Princetown and its Prison (Rev. L. Woollacombe).

Dartmoor Prison Past and Present (Captain V. Harris). W.Brendon & Sons.

Convict Life (Ticket of Leave Man). Wyman & Sons 1879.

Dartmoor Prison (A.J.Rhodes).

A Prisoner's Memoires (Charles Andrews). New York 1852.

Victorian Prison Lives (P.Priestly). Methuen, London. 1985

Out of the Blue (W. Hutchings).

The Beat on Western Dartmoor (S. Dell, M.B.E.). Forest Publishing.

The Truth About Dartmoor (George Dendrickson & Frederick Thomas).
     Victor Gollancz Ltd.

My Story (R. Kray). Pan Books

Westcountry Studies Library, Exeter.

West Devon Record Office, Coxside, Plymouth.

Local Studies Library, Plymouth.

Public Record Office, Kew, Surrey.

National Motor Museum, Beaulieu, Hants. (Curator: Mr. M. Ware).

Dartmoor Prison Museum, Princetown. (Curator: Mr. B. Johnson).

Devon and Cornwall Constabulary Museum, Exeter. (Curator: Mr. B. Estill).